Student Study Guide

Ellen G. Cohn, Ph.D.
Florida International University

CRIMINOLOGY TODAY

AN INTEGRATIVE INTRODUCTION

THIRD EDITION

FRANK SCHMALLEGER, PH.D.
Professor Emeritus, The University of North Carolina at Pembroke

Upper Saddle River, New Jersey 07458

Copyright © 2002, 1999, 1996 by Pearson Education, Inc., Upper Saddle River, New Jersey 07458. All rights reserved. Printed in the United States of America. This publication is protected by Copyright and permission should be obtained from the publisher prior to any prohibited reproduction, storage in a retrieval system, or transmission in any form or by any means, electronic, mechanical, photocopying, recording, or likewise. For information regarding permission(s), write to: Rights and Permissions Department.

10 9 8 7 6 5 4 3 2
ISBN 0-13-093677-4

contents

Introduction iv

PART I   THE CRIME PICTURE

Chapter 1   What Is Criminology?   1
Chapter 2   Patterns of Crime   13
Chapter 3   Research Methods and Theory Development   29

PART II   CRIME CAUSATION

Chapter 4   Classical and Neoclassical Thought   41
Chapter 5   Biological Roots of Criminal Behavior   55
Chapter 6   Psychological and Psychiatric Foundations of Criminal Behavior   67
Chapter 7   Sociological Theories I: Social Structure   81
Chapter 8   Sociological Theories II: Social Process and Social Development   93
Chapter 9   Sociological Theories III: Social Conflict   107

PART III   CRIME IN THE MODERN WORLD

Chapter 10   Crimes against Persons   119
Chapter 11   Crimes against Property   133
Chapter 12   White-Collar and Organized Crime   146
Chapter 13   Drug Abuse and Crime   155
Chapter 14   Technology and Crime   169

PART IV   RESPONDING TO CRIMINAL BEHAVIOR

Chapter 15   Criminology and Social Policy   181
Chapter 16   Future Directions   195

Answers to Odd-Numbered Questions   203

introduction

Welcome to the field of criminology! This study guide has been designed to supplement your textbook, Frank Schmalleger's, *Criminology Today*. It is not intended to be a substitute for reading and studying the textbook! Please read each chapter in the textbook in addition to using the study guide. To get the most out of both your textbook and study guide, you may want to follow these steps when studying each chapter:

1. First, review the learning objectives, which are found in both the textbook and the study guide. They provide you with goals so keep them in mind while you study the chapter.
2. Next, read through the chapter summary provided in the study guide to obtain an overview of the chapter's contents. Remember—reading the summary is not the same as reading the chapter!
3. Carefully read the chapter in your textbook. While reading, keep in mind the various issues raised in the learning objectives. You may choose to use the chapter outline section in your study guide to take notes while reading the chapter.
4. Review the key concepts found in your study guide. Use them to solve the Word Search and Crossword Puzzles in the study guide.
5. Try to complete the student study guide questions (found in the study guide) without referring back to the text for help. This self-test includes true/false, fill-in-the-blank, and multiple choice questions. This will help you determine how well you have learned the material in this chapter. If you do not do well on the self-test, you may want to review the chapter and study guide materials again.

The study guide also contains one or more student exercises in each chapter. Your professor may assign these as homework or extra credit assignments. It also includes a list of related web sites. You may wish to explore these sites to obtain more information on the topics covered in the chapter.

On a personal note, I hope that you will find this study guide both helpful and enjoyable. If you have any suggestions or ideas as to how this manual may be improved, please feel free to contact me. Enjoy your study of criminology!

Ellen G. Cohn, Ph.D.
Florida International University
author@crimtoday.com

what is criminology?

Learning Objectives

After reading this chapter, you should be able to:

1. Understand what criminology is and what criminologists do
2. Define crime
3. Recognize the difference between criminal and deviant acts, and appreciate the complexity of this distinction
4. Understand the legalistic approach to the study of crime and know why it is limiting
5. Know what a theory is and explain the role of theorizing in the study of criminal behavior
6. Understand the distinction between the social problems and social responsibility perspectives on crime causation

CHAPTER 1

CHAPTER SUMMARY

This Chapter provides an introduction to the textbook and to the field of criminology. It begins by discussing various perspectives for defining crime, including the legal, political, sociological, and psychological viewpoints. The definition used in the text is from the legal perspective, which sees crime as "human conduct in violation of the criminal laws of a state, the federal government, or a local jurisdiction that has the power to make such laws." This approach does have some limitations, however, some of which may be addressed by the other perspectives on crime.

While many crimes are forms of deviant behavior, behavior that violates social norms, not all crimes are deviant and not all deviant behavior is criminal. There is also a significant difference between what is criminal and what should be criminal. The consensus perspective holds that a law should be developed to criminalize a certain behavior when the members of a society generally agree that such a law is necessary. However, in a multicultural society, consensus may be difficult to achieve. The diversity of society is recognized in the pluralistic perspective which suggests that behaviors are typically criminalized through a political process after debate over the appropriate course of action. The issue of medical marijuana is an example of this process.

This chapter also discusses what a criminologist is, and considers the differences between a criminologist, a criminalist, and a criminal justice professional. Various professional opportunities for individuals with degrees in criminology are explored. The field of criminology itself is also discussed in detail, with various definitions considered. While criminology is primarily a social science, it is interdisciplinary. It contributes to, and overlaps, the field of criminal justice. One subfield is theoretical criminology, which posits explanations for criminal behavior. The chapter compares general and integrated theories of crime.

The development of social polices based on research findings may be of broader importance to society than theory testing. The chapter discusses how research into the effect of the media on teenage violence has been incorporated into federal reports and how it may eventually affect the development of new legislation regulating media programming. Concern over crime is one of the key issues in the country, making it an important determinant of public policy.

The social policy theme of the text is expanded through a contrast of the two main perspectives popular in today's society: the social problems perspective and the social responsibility perspective. The case of Jesse Timmendequas is discussed as an example of the contrast between these two perspectives. Recently, the social responsibility perspective has had a substantial influence on national crime control policy.

Crime is seen as a social event rather than as an isolated individual activity. The criminal event is the result of the coming together of inputs provided by the offender, the victim, the criminal justice system, and the general public (society). Background and foreground features or inputs provided by each contributor are discussed. In addition, each crime has consequences, or outputs, which affect not only the victim and offender but also society and the criminal justice system. These consequences may be immediate or more long-term.

This text recognizes the primacy of sociology: the belief that the primary perspective from which many contemporary criminologists operate is a sociological one. However, not all criminologists agree with this perspective and new and emerging perspectives are being developed.

KEY CONCEPTS

crime Human conduct in violation of the criminal laws of a state, the federal government, or a local jurisdiction that has the power to make such laws.

criminalist A specialist in the collection and examination of the physical evidence of crime.

Chapter 1 What Is Criminology?

criminality A behavioral predisposition that disproportionately favors criminal activity.

criminalize To make illegal.

criminal justice The scientific study of crime, the criminal law, and components of the criminal justice system, including the police, courts, and corrections.

criminal justice system The various agencies of justice, especially the police, courts, and corrections, whose goal it is to apprehend, convict, punish, and rehabilitate law violators.

criminologist One who is trained in the field of criminology. Also, one who studies crime, criminals, and criminal behavior.

criminology An interdisciplinary profession built around the scientific study of crime and criminal behavior, including their forms, causes, legal aspects, and control.

deviant behavior Behavior that violates social norms or is statistically different from the "average."

general theory A theory that attempts to explain all (or at least most) forms of criminal conduct through a single, overarching approach.

integrated theory An explanatory perspective that merges (or attempts to merge) concepts drawn from different sources.

Socialization The lifelong process of social experience whereby individuals acquire the cultural patterns of their society.

social policy A government initiative, program, or plan intended to address problems in society. The "war on crime," for example, is a kind of generic (large-scale) social policy-one consisting of many smaller programs.

social problems perspective The belief that crime is a manifestation of underlying social problems, such as poverty, discrimination, pervasive family violence, inadequate socialization practices, and the breakdown of traditional social institutions.

social relativity The notion that social events are differently interpreted according to the cultural experiences and personal interests of the initiator, the observer, or the recipient of that behavior.

social responsibility perspective The belief that individuals are fundamentally responsible for their own behavior and that they choose crime over other, more law-abiding, courses of action.

statutory law Law in the form of statutes or formal written strictures made by a legislature or governing body with the power to make law.

theory A series of interrelated propositions that attempt to describe, explain, predict, and ultimately control some class of events. A theory gains explanatory power from inherent logical consistency and is "tested" by how well it describes and predicts reality. (1; 3)

unicausal Having one cause. Unicausal theories posit only one source for all that they attempt to explain.

Part 1 The Crime Picture

CHAPTER OUTLINE

I. Introduction _____
_____

II. What Is Crime? _____
_____

III. Crime and Deviance _____
_____

IV. What Should Be Criminal? _____
_____

V. What Do Criminologists Do? _____
_____

VI. What Is Criminology? _____
_____

A. Theoretical Criminology _____
_____

VII. Criminology and Social Policy _____
_____

A. Social Policy and Public Crime Concerns _____
_____

VIII. The Theme of This Book _____
_____

IX. The Social Context of Crime _____
_____

A. Making Sense of Crime: The Causes and Consequences of the Criminal Event __
_____

X. The Primacy of Sociology? _____
_____

DISCUSSION QUESTIONS

These discussion questions are found in the textbook at the end of the chapter. Your instructor may want to focus on these questions during your coverage of Chapter 1.

1. This book emphasizes a social problems versus social responsibility theme. Describe both perspectives. How might social policy decisions based on these perspectives vary?

2. What is *crime*? What is the difference between crime and deviance? How might the notion of crime change over time? What impact does the changing nature of crime hold for criminology?

Chapter 1 What Is Criminology?

3. Do you believe that doctor-assisted suicide should be legalized? Why or why not? What do such crimes as doctor-assisted suicide have to tell us about the nature of the law and about crime in general?

4. Do you think that policymakers should address crime as a matter of individual responsibility and accountability, or do you think that crime is truly a symptom of a dysfunctional society? Why?

5. Describe the various participants in a criminal event. How does each contribute to an understanding of the event?

6. What do criminologists do? Do you think you might want to become a criminologist? Why or why not?

7. Why is the sociological perspective especially important in studying crime? What other perspectives might be relevant? Why?

STUDENT EXERCISES

Activity 1

Watch a number of reality-based television shows such as *Cops* and keep a record of the following information for each crime/event:

1. The gender and race of the suspects

2. The gender and race of the police officers

3. The type of crime

4. The products being advertised during these programs

Questions to consider:

1. What is the predominant race of the suspects? The police officers?

2. Do you notice any difference in the behavior of the suspects and police officers when they are both of the same race? Of different races? Of different genders?

3. What types of crimes are featured? Does one type of crime predominate?

4. Are the products advertised during these programs directed toward any specific subgroup of the population? Are they age- or gender-based?

Activity 2

First, identify five behaviors that are against the law but which you do not consider to be deviant, as well as five legal behaviors which you consider to be deviant. Your instructor will divide the class into groups. Within each group, compare and contrast the items on your lists. Focus on the wide range of opinions present among a fairly homogeneous group (university students studying criminal justice). Discuss possible reasons for differing opinions (e.g., religious beliefs, profession, prior experiences with the criminal justice system).

CRIMINOLOGY TODAY ON THE WEB

http://www.talkjustice.com/cybrary.asp

This site is maintained by the author of your textbook, Dr. Frank Schmalleger, and includes an extensive collection of links to criminal justice and criminology Web sites.

http://www.criminology.fsu.edu/cjlinks

This is Dr. Cecil Greek's Criminal Justice Links, which includes a huge number of links to all sorts of criminology- and criminal justice-related Web sites.

Chapter 1   What Is Criminology?

http://faculty.ncwc.edu/toconnor/linklist.htm

This is the Criminal Justice Mega-Sites Web page, which includes an annotated list of criminology and criminal justice sites.

PRACTICE QUESTIONS

True/False

_____ 1. Random violent stranger attacks are the most feared type of crime.

_____ 2. The legalistic perspective defines crime as conduct in violation of the criminal law.

_____ 3. The political perspective defines crime in terms of popular notions of right and wrong.

_____ 4. A unified definition of crime is simple to achieve.

_____ 5. All criminal behavior is deviant.

_____ 6. The pluralistic perspective is most applicable to societies characterized by a shared belief system.

_____ 7. Criminology is an interdisciplinary field.

_____ 8. Theoretical criminology focuses on describing crime and its occurrence.

_____ 9. Concern over crime is no longer a serious issue in the United States.

_____ 10. Concern over crime is not necessarily related to the actual incidence of crime.

_____ 11. According to the text, crime is an isolated individual activity.

Fill in the Blank

12. The _____ perspective sees crime as human conduct that violates the criminal law.

13. Criminalization involves making some forms of behavior _____.

14. The psychological perspective is also known as the _____ perspective.

15. _____ is human behavior that violates social norms.

16. A _____ specializes in the collection and examination of the physical evidence of crime.

17. The term *criminology* was coined by _____.

18. Criminology contributes to the discipline of _____.

19. _____ has been attributed to films and television.

20. The social problems perspective is characteristic of what social scientists term a _____ approach.

21. The primacy of sociology emphasizes that crime is a _____.

Multiple Choice

22. The type of crime that people fear most involves a
    a. violent crime committed by a stranger.
    b. nonviolent crime committed by a stranger.
    c. violent crime committed by a member of the family.
    d. nonviolent crime committed by a member of the family.

23. "Human conduct that is in violation of the criminal laws of a state, the federal government, or a local jurisdiction that has the power to make such laws" is a definition of
    a. criminology.
    b. crime.
    c. criminal.
    d. deviance.

24. The process of _____ involves making some forms of behavior illegal.
    a. criminalization
    b. legalization
    c. common law
    d. decriminalization

25. The belief that crime is an antisocial act of such a nature that repression is necessary to preserve the existing system of society is the basis of the _____ perspective on crime.
    a. legal
    b. political
    c. sociological
    d. psychological

26. _____ is human behavior that violates social norms or is statistically different from the average.
    a. Crime
    b. Deviance
    c. Cruelty
    d. Adaptive behavior

27. Because you were late for this exam, you exceeded the speed limit by about 10 to 15 miles per hour while driving to class. This is an example of behavior that is
    a. deviant but not criminal.
    b. criminal but not deviant.
    c. both deviant and criminal.
    d. neither deviant nor criminal.

28. The medical marijuana debate is an example of the _____ perspective.
    a. consensus
    b. psychological
    c. sociological
    d. pluralistic

29. One who studies crime, criminals, and criminal behavior is called a
    a. scientist.
    b. criminal justice professional.
    c. criminologist.
    d. criminalism.

30. The official publication of the American Society of Criminology is
    a. *Criminology.*
    b. *Justice Quarterly.*
    c. *The Journal of Quantitative Criminology.*
    d. *Crime and Delinquency.*

Chapter 1   What Is Criminology?

31. Because it draws on other fields to understand the problem of crime, criminology is considered a(n) _____ field.
    a. unified
    b. integrated
    c. interdisciplinary
    d. professional

32. The field of study that is concerned primarily with the causes and consequences of crime is
    a. criminology.
    b. criminal justice.
    c. criminality.
    d. criminalistics.

33. A(n) _____ theory does not necessarily attempt to explain all criminality.
    a. general
    b. integrated
    c. unicausal
    d. complete

34. Workplace homicide is
    a. the fastest-growing type of murder in the United States.
    b. the leading cause of workplace death for women.
    c. both a and b
    d. none of the above

35. The social problems perspective holds that crime is
    a. a manifestation of underlying social problems.
    b. chosen by individual perpetrators.
    c. not going to be solved by social programs.
    d. none of the above

36. Which of the following crime reduction or prevention strategies is most characteristic of the social problems perspective?
    a. A government-funded initiative to enhance educational opportunities among low-income individuals
    b. A move to broaden police powers by increasing the number of exceptions to the Exclusionary Rule
    c. Rewriting state statutes to increase the severity of punishment for violent offenders, such as three-strikes laws
    d. All of the above

37. Which of the following is not a foreground contribution by an offender?
    a. A particular motivation
    b. A peculiar biology
    c. A specific intent
    d. A drug-induced state of mind

38. A victim may actively contribute to his/her own victimization through the appearance of
    a. defensiveness.
    b. exposure.
    c. defenselessness.
    d. precipitation.

WORD SEARCH PUZZLE

Common law
Crime
Criminalist
Criminality
Criminalize
Criminologist
Deviance
Integrated
Socialization
Statute
Theory
Unicausal

```
Y L S O C E J C L L C R C X L
G A O T J R K B J C R R Q T N
O S C R I M I N A L I S T T U
W U I M T O S M Y M M P V H C
S A A F R Q E P I X I V B Y Y
E C L I U T M N J N N L B R T
V I I N U K O C Y N A A G O K
X N Z T O L Y D X M L L N E D
I U A E O M E K B J I B I H M
S T T G Z V M Y E J Z C I T O
S K I R I R I O T D E R O D Y
W S O A E S R T C H M Z X X B
T X N T M S C L D S U V I O T
O C Y E C P W Z D G T U Q Z O
E I H D G G R Y M X O T W G F
```

Chapter 1 What Is Criminology?

CROSSWORD PUZZLE

Across

2. Law in the form of formal written strictures. (2 words)
3. To make a behavior illegal.
6. Someone who studies crime and criminals.
7. A behavioral predisposition that favors criminal activity disproportionally.
8. A series of propositions that describe, explain, predict, and control events.

Down

1. Behavior that violates social norms.
2. The lifelong process of social experience whereby individuals acquire cultural patterns.
3. Someone who collects and examines the physical evidence of a crime.
4. Human conduct in violation of the criminal laws of a state or the federal government.
5. A codified law.

patterns of crime

Learning Objectives

After reading this chapter, you should be able to:

1. Explain the history of statistical crime data collection and analysis, and understand the usefulness and limitations of crime data
2. Recognize the various methods currently in use to collect and disseminate crime data
3. Describe and explain the major sources of crime data in the United States, including the UCR, the NIBRS, and the NCVS
4. Define and discuss the social dimensions of crime, including key demographic factors
5. Discuss the economic costs of crime

CHAPTER 2

CHAPTER SUMMARY

This chapter describes various sources of crime statistics. The two primary sources of information on crime in the United States today are official statistics and victimization statistics. Official statistics are found in the FBI's *Uniform Crime Reports* (UCR) and National Incident-Based Reporting System (NIBRS). Both are compiled annually by the FBI and contain data provided by police departments around the country. However, official statistics only include information on crimes known to the police and provide no insight into the dark figure of unreported crime. Victimization statistics, as provided by the National Crime Victimization Survey (NCVS), seek to obtain information on unreported crime. Subjects in the survey are asked about their victimization experiences; information is collected on the crime, the offender, and the specific incident, including whether or not the victim reported the criminal event to the police. Both sources of information have limitations.

The text also discusses the eight Part I or index offenses defined by the UCR. These include murder, forcible rape, aggravated assault, robbery, burglary, larceny/theft, motor vehicle theft, and arson. Information about these crimes obtained from the UCR and the NCVS is presented.

Information on the dark figure of crime may also be obtained from self-report surveys, in which anonymous respondents are asked to report confidentially any crimes they may have committed. The best known such surveys include the National Youth Survey, which surveys juveniles between the ages of 11 and 17, and the *Monitoring the Future* study, which focuses on the behaviors, attitudes, and values of students and young adults in the United States.

The social dimensions of crime are aspects of crime and victimization that relate to socially significant attributes by which groups are defined. These include age, gender, ethnicity, and social class. Criminal activity is associated more with youth, and most forms of criminality decrease with age (the desistance phenomenon). Elderly offenders are more likely to commit crimes requiring special skills and knowledge. The elderly are less likely to be victimized than any other group. Gender may be the best single predictor of criminality, with males being much more likely than women to commit most crimes. Women are also victimized less frequently than men in most crime categories (with the exceptions of the crimes of rape and spouse abuse).

Ethnicity may also be related to crime; arrest rates of blacks are significantly higher than their proportion in the population. The question of whether the criminal justice system is racist is discussed. Blacks are also more likely to be victimized than whites; the high rates of both crime and criminal victimization within the black community have led to a heightened fear of crime among blacks in the United States. The relationship of social class to crime originally assumed to exist began to be questioned in the 1960s. Recent data from the National Youth Survey does suggest that a fairly significant correlation between criminality and social class exists, with members of lower social classes being more likely to be involved in serious street crimes.

The overall cost of crime is difficult to measure. Costs to the victim may include medical treatment and/or hospitalization, the loss of valued property, psychological trauma, loss of work time, increased insurance premiums, and various intangible costs such as pain and suffering.

KEY CONCEPTS

aggravated assault (UCR) An unlawful attack by one person upon another for the purpose of inflicting severe or aggravated bodily injury. See also simple assault.

arson The willful or malicious burning or attempt to burn, with or without intent to defraud, of a dwelling house, public building, motor vehicle or aircraft, personal property of another, and so on.

burglary By the narrowest and oldest definition, the trespassory breaking and entering of the dwelling house of another in the nighttime with the intent to commit a felony. Also, the unlawful entry of a structure to commit a felony or a theft.

burglary (UCR) The unlawful entry of any fixed structure, vehicle, or vessel used for regular residence, industry, or business, with or without force, with intent to commit a felony or a larceny.

carjacking The stealing of a car while it is occupied.

clearance rate The proportion of reported or discovered crimes within a given offense category that are solved.

cohort A group of individuals having certain significant social characteristics in common, such as gender and date and place of birth.

correlation A causal, complementary, or reciprocal relationship between two measurable variables. See also **statistical correlation**.

criminal homicide (UCR) The UCR category which includes and is limited to all offenses of causing the death of another person without justification or excuse.

criminality index The actual extent of the crime problem in a society. The criminality index is computed by adding the actual crime rate and the latent crime rate.

dark figure of crime The numerical total of unreported crimes that are not reflected in official crime statistics.

date rape Unlawful forced sexual intercourse with a woman against her will which occurs within the context of a dating relationship.

demographics The characteristics of population groups, usually expressed in statistical fashion.

desistance phenomenon The observable decrease in crime rates that is invariably associated with age.

felony murder A special class of criminal homicide in which an offender may be charged with first-degree murder when that person's criminal activity results in another person's death.

first-degree murder Criminal homicide that is planned or involves premeditation.

forcible rape (UCR) The carnal knowledge of a female forcibly and against her will. Assaults or attempts to commit rape by force or threat of force are also included in the UCR definition; however, statutory rape (without force) and other sex offenses are excluded.

hate crime A criminal offense in which the motive is hatred, bias, or prejudice based on the actual or perceived race, color, religion, national origin, ethnicity, gender, or sexual orientation of another individual or group of individuals. Also called bias crime.

homicide The killing of one human being by another.

household crime (NCVS) An attempted or completed crime that does not involve confrontation such as burglary, motor vehicle theft, and household larceny.

larceny The unlawful taking or attempted taking of property (other than a motor vehicle) from the possession of another, by stealth, without force or deceit, with intent to permanently deprive the owner of the property.

larceny-theft (UCR) The unlawful taking, carrying, leading, or riding away of property (other than a motor vehicle) from the possession or constructive possession of another. Attempts are included.

latent crime rate A rate of crime calculated on the basis of crimes that would likely be committed by those who are in prison or jail or who are otherwise incapacitated by the justice system.

mass murder The illegal killing of four or more victims at one location within one event.

Monitoring the Future (MTF) A national self-report survey on drug use that has been conducted since 1975.

motor vehicle theft (UCR) The theft or attempted theft of a motor vehicle. According to the Federal Bureau of Investigation, this offense category includes the stealing of automobiles, trucks, buses, motorcycles, motorscooters, and snowmobiles.

murder An unlawful homicide.

National Crime Victimization Survey (NCVS) A survey conducted annually by the Bureau of Justice Statistics that provides data on surveyed households that report they were affected by crime.

National Incident-Based Reporting System (NIBRS) A new and enhanced statistical reporting system that will collect data on each single incident and arrest within 22 crime categories.

National Youth Survey (NYS) A longitudinal panel study of a national sample of 1,725 individuals that measured self-reports of delinquency and other types of behavior.

negligent homicide The act of causing the death of another person by recklessness or gross negligence.

Part I offense Any of a group of offenses, also called "major offenses" or "index offenses," for which the UCR publishes counts of reported instances. Part I offenses consist of murder, rape, robbery, aggravated assault, burglary, larceny, auto theft, and arson.

Part II offense Any of a set of UCR categories used to report data concerning arrests for less serious offenses.

rape (NCVS) Carnal knowledge through the use of force or the threat of force, including attempts. Statutory rape (without force) is excluded. Both heterosexual and homosexual rape are included.

robbery (UCR) The taking or attempting to take anything of value from the care, custody, or control of a person or persons by force or threat of force or violence or by putting the victim in fear.

second-degree murder criminal homicide that is unplanned and is often described as a "crime of passion."

self-report survey A survey in which anonymous respondents, without fear of disclosure or arrest, are asked to confidentially report any violations of the criminal law that they have committed.

Chapter 2 Patterns of Crime

serial murder Criminal homicide which involves the killing of several victims in three or more separate events.

simple assault (NCVS) An attack without a weapon resulting either in minor injury or in undetermined injury requiring less than two days of hospitalization. See also **aggravated assault**.

statistical school) A criminological perspective with roots in the early 1800s which seeks to uncover correlations between crime rates and other types of demographic data.

superpredator One of a new generation of juveniles "who are coming of age in actual and 'moral poverty' without the benefits of parents, teachers, coaches and clergy to teach them right from wrong and show them 'unconditional love.'"[1] The term is often applied to inner-city youths who meet the criteria it sets forth.

Uniform Crime Reporting Program A Federal Bureau of Investigation summation of crime statistics tallied annually and consisting primarily of data on crimes reported to the police and of arrests.

victimization rate (NCVS) A measure of the occurrence of victimizations among a specified population group. For personal crimes, the rate is based on the number of victimizations per 1,000 residents aged 12 or older. For household crimes, the victimization rates are calculated using the number of incidents per 1,000 households.

CHAPTER OUTLINE

I. Introduction _____

II. A History of Crime Statistics _____

    A. Adolphe Quételet and André Michel Guerry _____

III. Crime Statistics Today _____

    A. Programmatic Problems with Available Data _____

    B. The UCR Program _____

    C. NIBRS: The New UCR_____

    D. Hate Crimes_____

    F. Data Gathering Under the NCVS _____

---

[1] See John J. DiIulio, Jr., "The Question of Black Crime," *Public Interest*, fall 1994, pp. 3-12. The term superpredator is generally attributed to DiIulio.

      G. Patterns of Change _____
      _____

      H. The Crime Problem _____
      _____

IV. Major Crimes _____
    _____

      A. Criminal Homicide _____
      _____

      B. Forcible Rape _____
      _____

      C. Robbery _____
      _____

      D. Aggravated Assault _____
      _____

      E. Burglary _____
      _____

      F. Larceny _____
      _____

      G. Motor Vehicle Theft _____
      _____

      H. Arson _____
      _____

V. Part II Offenses _____
    _____

VI. Other Sources of Data _____
    _____

VII. Unreported Crime _____
    _____

VIII. The Social Dimensions of Crime _____
    _____

      A. What Are "Social Dimensions"? _____
      _____

      B. Age and Crime _____
      _____

      C. Gender and Crime _____
      _____

Chapter 2 Patterns of Crime

      D. Ethnicity and Crime _____

      _____

      E. Social Class and Crime _____

      _____

IX. The Costs of Crime _____

_____

DISCUSSION QUESTIONS

These discussion questions are found in the textbook at the end of the chapter. The instructor may want to focus on these questions at the conclusion of the lecture on Chapter 2.

1. This book emphasizes a social problems versus social responsibility theme. Which perspective is best supported by a realistic appraisal of the "social dimensions" of crime discussed in this chapter? Explain.

2. What are the major differences between the NCVS, the UCR, and NIBRS? Can useful comparisons be made among these programs? If so, what comparisons?

3. What does it mean to say that the UCR is summary-based, while the NIBRS is incident based? When NIBRS is fully operational, what kinds of data will it contribute to the UCR program? How will this information be useful?

4. What is a *crime rate*? How are rates useful? How might the NCVS, UCR, and NIBRS make better use of rates?

5. Why don't victims report crimes to the police? Which crimes appear to be the least frequently reported? Why are those crimes so rarely reported? Which crimes appear to be the most frequently reported? Why are they so often reported?

6. Is the extent of the crime problem in this country accurately assessed by the statistical data available through the UCR/NIBRS and the NCVS? Why or why not?

7. This chapter discusses losses due to crime. Can you think of any ways in which "losses due to crime" might be measured other than those discussed here? If so, how?

8. This chapter says that black people appear to be overrepresented in many categories of criminal activity. Do you believe that the statistics cited in this chapter accurately reflect the degree of black/white involvement in crime? Why or why not? How might they be inaccurate?

STUDENT EXERCISES

Activity 1

This activity involves comparing the definitions used by the FBI with those used by state criminal codes.

1. Obtain the definitions used by the FBI for each of the eight Part I offenses. This information is available on the World Wide Web at the FBI's Web site (http://www.fbi.gov/ucr/ucr.htm).

2. Obtain the definitions of the same eight crimes for your state. One way to locate state statutes on the Web is to access the Cornell University School of Law's Legal Information Institute site at http://www.law.cornell.edu/statutes.html. (Note: Your instructor may choose to assign you a different state.)

3. Compare and contrast the definitions used by the FBI with those of your state. What differences do you see?

Activity 2

Your instructor will assign you two large cities in the United States and one index offense (e.g., burglary). Go to the FBI's Web site and access the most recent UCR data for these two cities. Answer the following questions:

1. Print out the number of burglaries known to the police for each of the two cities.

Chapter 2 Patterns of Crime

2. Which city had more reported burglaries?

3. What were the burglary rates for each of the two cities?

4. Did the burglary rates change over time in either city?

5. What factors might explain the differences in the burglary rates?

CRIMINOLOGY TODAY ON THE WEB

http://www.fbi.gov/ucr/ucr.htm

This Web site will provide you with access to recent issues of the Uniform Crime Reports as well as information on the National Incident-Based Reporting System and other statistics collected by the FBI.

http://www.ojp.usdoj.gov/bjs

This is the home page for the Bureau of Justice Statistics. From here you can access recent issues of the *National Crime Victimization Survey* as well as data from many other sources.

http://www.albany.edu/sourcebook

This Web site provides a link to the *Sourcebook of Criminal Justice Statistics*, which is published by the Bureau of Justice Statistics and includes data from many sources, covering many aspects of the U.S. criminal justice system.

http://www.law.cornell.edu

This is the site of the Legal Information Institute of the Cornell University School of Law. It includes links to federal and state constitutions, statutes, and codes of law.

PRACTICE QUESTIONS

True/False

_____ 1. The collection of population statistics is a relatively new phenomenon.

_____ 2. The UCR program was begun by the FBI in 1929.

_____ 3. The UCR program may seriously overestimate the true incidence of crime in the United States.

_____ 4. Hate crimes are most commonly perpetrated against an individual.

_____ 5. According to the NCVS, young people are more likely to be victimized than older people.

_____ 6. The actual occurrence of all crimes that are reported to NCVS interviewers is verified before they are included in the data.

_____ 7. Second-degree murder involves the concept of malice aforethought.

_____ 8. Murder is primarily an interracial crime.

_____ 9. According to the NCVS, stranger rapes are more common than rapes by nonstrangers.

_____ 10. The number of reported aggravated assaults is decreasing, according to the UCR.

_____ 11. Self-report surveys provide information on the dark figure of crime.

_____ 12. Fear of future victimization is one of the most common reasons for not reporting a violent victimization to the police.

_____ 13. Correlation does not imply causation.

_____ 14. Criminal activity is most associated with youth than with any other stage of life.

_____ 15. According to the National Youth Survey, there is no correlation between criminality and social class.

_____ 16. According to the NCVS, black women aged 65 or older have the lowest violent crime victimization rates.

Fill in the Blank

17. Inferences based on statistical _____ appear to be a product of the last 200 years.

18. Unreported criminal activity is known as the _____.

19. According to the NCVS, approximately _____ of all violent crimes are reported to the police.

20. _____ is the wilful killing of one human being by another.

21. _____ has the highest clearance rate of any index offense.

22. According to the UCR, in 1999, the month of _____ showed the largest number of reported forcible rapes.

23. The _____ established campus crime statistic reporting requirements for universities receiving any form of federal funding.

24. A(n) _____ is a connection or association observed to exist between two measurable variables.

25. The murder rate among blacks is _____ times that of whites.

Multiple Choice

26. The thermic law of crime was developed by
    a. André Michel Guerry.
    b. Cesare Beccaria.
    c. Adolphe Quételet.
    d. Thomas Robert Malthus.

Chapter 2 Patterns of Crime

27. The _____ definition of rape excludes homosexual rape.
    a. Uniform Crime Reports
    b. National Incident-Based Reporting System
    c. National Crime Victimization Survey
    d. U.S. Code

28. UCR Part I offenses are subdivided into two categories:
    a. felonies and misdemeanors.
    b. violent crimes and personal crimes.
    c. violent personal crimes and property crimes.
    d. violent personal crimes and index crimes.

29. The proportion of reported or discovered crime within a given offense category which is solved by the police is known as the _____ rate.
    a. arrest
    b. index
    c. clearance
    d. indictment

30. Which of the following is not a NIBRS Group A offense?
    a. Pornography
    b. Kidnapping
    c. Gambling offenses
    d. Disorderly conduct

31. Hate crimes are most commonly committed by
    a. black males.
    b. black females.
    c. white males.
    d. white females.

32. According to the NCVS, members of which racial group are most likely to be victimized?
    a. Whites
    b. Blacks
    c. Hispanics
    d. Asians

33. Which of the following individuals is most likely to be the victim of a violent crime?
    a. A young black male
    b. A young black female
    c. A young white male
    d. A young white female

34. Official crime rates in the United States are_____; correctional populations are _____.
    a. decreasing; increasing
    b. decreasing; decreasing
    c. increasing, decreasing
    d. increasing; increasing

35. _____ is legally seen as a true crime of passion.
    a. First-degree murder
    b. Second-degree murder
    c. Third-degree murder
    d. Negligent homicide

36. The Columbine High School shooting is an example of
    a. serial murder.
    b. spree murder.
    c. mass murder.
    d. none of the above

37. Mike Tyson was convicted of the index offense of
    a. homicide.
    b. forcible rape.
    c. robbery.
    d. none of the above

38. According to the UCR, the rate of reported forcible rape is highest in the _____ months.
    a. summer
    b. spring
    c. winter
    d. fall

39. According to the UCR, the most common month for robbery is
    a. January.
    b. July.
    c. September.
    d. December.

40. If you unlawfully enter a structure to commit a felony, you have probably committed the crime of
    a. theft.
    b. robbery.
    c. burglary.
    d. breaking and entering.

41. According to UCR larceny statistics, most items reported stolen were taken from
    a. buildings.
    b. coin-operated machines.
    c. parked cars.
    d. private residences.

42. Vanity pyromaniacs commit arson because they
    a. suffer from psychological problems.
    b. are trying to take credit for putting out the fire they originally started.
    c. are trying to defraud an insurance company.
    d. are attempting to disguise another felony, such as burglary or murder.

43. Which of the following is not a finding of the National Youth Survey?
    a. Females are involved in a smaller proportion of crime than previously thought.
    b. Violent offenders begin lives of crime earlier than originally believed.
    c. Race differentials in crime are smaller than traditional data sources indicated.
    d. There is a consistent progression from less serious to more serious acts of delinquency over time.

44. One of the two most common reasons for not reporting violent crime is that
    a. the victim fears future victimization by the same offender.
    b. the victim believes the police will be ineffective in solving the crime.
    c. the victim is embarrassed over the type of victimization.
    d. the victim considers the crime to be a private matter.

Chapter 2   Patterns of Crime

45. Older offenders are more likely to commit
    a. assault.
    b. theft.
    c. street crimes.
    d. fraud.

46. The *Myth of a Racist Criminal Justice System* was written by
    a. Marvin D. Free, Jr.
    b. William Wilbanks.
    c. James Fox.
    d. Coramae Richey Mann.

WORD SEARCH PUZZLE

- Arson
- Burglary
- Carjacking
- Clearance
- Correlation
- Date rape
- Demographics
- Desistance
- Hate crime
- Homicide
- Murder
- NCVS
- NIBRS
- Rape
- Robbery
- Superpredator
- UCR

```
R C U E V W V D X T A I X J J
S O S X S C L E A R A N C E J
Y R T C C X J M S T S B L Q O
T R S A E Y L O F S E U M Q I
B E J R D R N G G J T R J A G
X L F J I E G R E H Z G A C V
K A N A C B R A M G F L Y P U
D T F C I B L P I F S A B E E
N I I K M O X H R E D R U M S
U O W I O R Z I C E N Y B A V
U N G N H W O C E O P C V I C
I Z U G Z A Y S T E B U Z G N
J A Q P L E C N A T S I S E D
F K M F A N U L H E U D I T P
```

Chapter 2 Patterns of Crime

CROSSWORD PUZZLE

Across

1. A survey conducted annually by the Bureau of Justice Statistics.
5. _____ murder involves the killing of several victims in three or more events.
6. Taking something of value from another person by force.
7. The characteristics of population groups.
9. Willful or malicious burning of a building.
10. The observable decrease in crime rates associated with age.
11. The willful killing of one human being by another.
12. Criminal homicide.
13. The unlawful entry of a structure to commit a felony or theft.

Down

2. A relationship between two measurable variables.
3. The proportion of crimes reported that are solved. (2 words)
4. A crime motivated by bias based on the victims race, color, religion, etc. (2 words)
8. Stealing a car while it is occupied.

research methods and theory development

CHAPTER 3

Learning Objectives

After reading this chapter, you should be able to:

1. Appreciate the relevance of criminological theory to the study of crime and criminals
2. Recognize the role of criminological research in theory development and display an understanding of various types of research designs
3. Identify research limitations, including problems in data collection and analysis
4. Recognize the ethical considerations involved in conducting criminological research.
5. Describe the process of writing the research report, and identify common sources for publishing research findings
6. Identify the impact of criminological research on the creation of social policy

CHAPTER SUMMARY

Criminological theory cannot be fully appreciated unless one understands its fundamental assumptions. This chapter examines how social scientific research methods are used in the development of criminological theories. A theory is a series of interrelated propositions which attempt to describe, explain, predict, and ultimately control some class of events, such as criminal behavior. Theories serve a variety of purposes and are tested through research, the use of standardized, systematic procedures in the search for knowledge. Research can be pure or applied, and can be primary or secondary. Research is conducted in four states: problem solving, research design development, the selection of data-gathering techniques, and a review of the findings.

Problem identification involves choosing a problem or issue to be studied. Much contemporary criminological research involves hypothesis testing. Research designs structure the research process. One basic design is the one-group pretest–posttest. However, this type of design does not eliminate the possibility of confounding effects, or rival explanations, which may affect both the internal and external validity of the research. The chapter lists a number of factors that may threaten the internal or external validity of a research design. The use of a controlled experiment or a quasi-experimental design may increase the validity of the results by eliminating some rival explanations. These designs require the use of randomization when assigning research subjects to experimental and control groups.

There are five main data-gathering strategies commonly used in criminology: survey research, case studies, participant observation, self-reporting, and secondary analysis. The strategy selected must produce information in a form usable to the researcher and thus depends on the questions to be answered. Data collection involves scientific observation, which must meet the criteria of intersubjectivity and replicability. Even so, some observations may lead to unwarranted conclusions. Once the data have been collected, they are usually analyzed in some way, generally using statistical techniques. Descriptive statistics, such as the mean, median, mode, and standard deviation, describe, summarize, and highlight the relationships within the data. Inferential statistics, including tests of significance, attempt to generalize findings by specifying how likely they are to be true for other populations or locations.

Research methods can be quantitative or qualitative. Both are useful and provide important information. Some criminologists believe that qualitative data-gathering strategies represent the future of criminological research.

Research is not conducted in a vacuum and cannot be free of biases and preconceptions. The best way to control biases is to be aware of them at the start of the research. Ethical issues are also extremely important; although they may not affect the validity of the results, they may have a significant impact upon the lives of researchers and subjects. Key ethical issues include protection of subjects from harm, privacy, disclosure, and data confidentiality. One way to overcome many of these ethical issues is through the use of informed consent. Criminological research may also have an impact on social policy, although many publicly elected officials may prefer to create politically expedient policies rather than consider current research.

After a research study has been conducted, the results are presented in the form of a research report or paper. There is a standard format which is generally followed. Most criminologists seek to publish their research results. The primary medium for such publication is refereed professional journals, which use peer reviewers to determine the quality of submitted manuscripts.

KEY CONCEPTS

applied research scientific inquiry that is designed and carried out with practical applications in mind.

Chapter 3 Research Methods and Theory Development

confounding effects A rival explanation, or competing hypothesis, which is a threat to the internal or external validity of a research design.

control group A group of experimental subjects which, although the subject of measurement and observation, is not exposed to the experimental intervention.

controlled experiments An experiment that attempts to hold conditions (other than the intentionally introduced experimental intervention) constant.

data confidentiality The ethical requirement of social scientific research to protect the confidentiality of individual research participants, while simultaneously preserving justified research access to the information participants provide.

descriptive statistics Statistics that describe, summarize, or highlight the relationships within data which have been gathered.

disclosure of research methods The provision of information to potential subjects informing them of the nature of the research methods to be used by the social scientific study in which their involvement is planned.

external validity The ability to generalize research findings to other settings.

heritability A statistical construct that estimates the amount of variation in a population that is attributable to genetic factors.

hypothesis An explanation that accounts for a set of facts and that can be tested by further investigation. Also, something that is taken to be true for the purpose of argument or investigation.[1]

inferential statistics Statistics that specify how likely findings are to be true for other populations or in other locales.

informed consent The ethical requirement of social scientific research that research subjects be informed as to the nature of the research about to be conducted, their anticipated role in it, and the uses to which the data they provide will be put.

internal validity The certainty that experimental interventions did indeed cause the changes observed in the study group. Also, the control over confounding factors which tend to invalidate the results of an experiment.

intersubjectivity A scientific principle which requires that independent observers see the same thing under the same circumstances for observations to be regarded as valid.

meta-analysis A study of other studies about a particular topic of interest.

operationalization The process by which concepts are made measurable.

participant observation A strategy in data gathering in which the researcher observes a group by participating, to varying degrees, in the activities of the group.[2]

primary research Research characterized by original and direct investigation.

pure research Research undertaken simply for the sake of advancing scientific knowledge.

---

1 *American Heritage Dictionary and Electronic Thesaurus.*
2 Frank E. Hagan, *Research Methods in Criminal Justice and Criminology* (New York: Macmillan, 1993), p. 103.

qualitative method A research technique that produces subjective results, or results that are difficult to quantify.

quantitative method A research technique that produces measurable results.

quasi-experimental design An approach to research which, although less powerful than experimental designs, is deemed worthy of use when better designs are not feasible.

randomization The process whereby individuals are assigned to study groups without biases or differences resulting from selection.

replicability (experimental) A scientific principle which holds that valid observations made at one time can be made again later if all other conditions are the same.

research The use of standardized, systematic procedures in the search for knowledge.[3]

research design The logic and structure inherent in an approach to data gathering.

secondary research New evaluations of existing information which had been collected by other researchers.

statistical correlation The simultaneous increase or decrease in value of two numerically valued random variables.

survey research A social science data-gathering technique which involves the use of questionnaires.

tests of significance A statistical technique intended to provide researchers with confidence that their results are in fact true and not the result of sampling error.

theory A series of interrelated propositions that attempt to describe, explain, predict, and ultimately control some class of events. A theory gains explanatory power from inherent logical consistency and is "tested" by how well it describes and predicts reality.

variable A concept that can undergo measurable changes.

verstehen The kind of subjective understanding that can be achieved by criminologists who immerse themselves in the everyday world of the criminals they study.

CHAPTER OUTLINE

I. Introduction _____

_____

II. The Science of Criminology _____

_____

III. Theory Building _____

_____

IV. The Role of Research _____

_____

    A. Problem Identification_____

_____

---

3 Abraham Kaplan, The *Conduct of Inquiry: Methodology for Behavioral Science* (San Francisco: Chandler, 1964), p. 71.
4 *American Heritage Dictionary and Electronic Thesaurus.*

Chapter 3 Research Methods and Theory Development　　　　　　　　　　　　　　　**33**

      B. Research Designs _____

      _____

      C. Techniques of Data Collection _____

      _____

      D. Data Analysis _____

      _____

  V. Quantitative versus Qualitative Methods _____

    _____

 VI. Values and Ethics in the Conduct of Research _____

    _____

VII. Social Policy and Criminological Research _____

    _____

VIII. Writing the Research Report _____

    _____

      A. Writing for Publication _____

      _____

DISCUSSION QUESTIONS

These discussion questions are found in the textbook at the end of the chapter. The instructor may want to focus on these questions at the conclusion of the lecture on Chapter 3.

1. This book emphasizes a social problems versus social responsibility theme. How might a thorough research agenda allow us to decide which perspective is most fruitful in combating crime?

2. What is a *hypothesis*? What does it mean to operationalize a hypothesis? Why is operationalization necessary?

3. What is a *theory*? Why is the task of criminological theory construction so demanding? How do we know if a theory is any good?

4. Explain experimental research. How might a good research design be diagrammed? What kinds of threats to the validity of research designs can you identify? How can such threats be controlled or eliminated?

5. List and describe the various types of data-gathering strategies discussed in this chapter. Is any one technique "better" than another? Why or why not? Under what kinds of conditions might certain types of data-gathering strategies be most appropriate?

6. What is the difference between qualitative and quantitative research? What are the advantages and disadvantages of each?

STUDENT EXERCISES

Activity 1

Many social science organizations have adopted official codes of ethics. This exercise deals with the similarities and differences found in the ethical codes of various fields.

1. First, go to the Academy of Criminal Justice Sciences (ACJS) home page at http://www.acjs.org and access the code of ethics. What (if anything) does the ACJS code of ethics have to say about each of the following?

    Informed consent

    Confidentiality

    Reporting of research

    Protection of subjects from harm

    Plagiarism

2. Then go to the home page of the American Society of Criminology (ASC) at http://www.asc41.com and access the ASC code of ethics. What does this code have to say about the subjects above?

Chapter 3 Research Methods and Theory Development

3. Finally, go to the home page of the American Sociological Association (ASA) at http://www.asanet.org and locate the ASA code of ethics. What does this code have to say about the subjects above?

4. Which of the three codes do you prefer, and why?

Activity 2

Aprilville, a small town outside Bigcity, plans to implement a Neighborhood Watch program. The town mayor has asked you to find out if the program, once implemented, will have any effect on the town's crime rate. Design a research study to answer this question:

1. Formulate one or more hypotheses and operationalize the concepts.

2. Choose a research design from those discussed in the chapter and explain why you selected this design.

3. Select a data-gathering strategy and explain why you chose this technique.

CRIMINOLOGY TODAY ON THE WEB

http://www.acjs.org
This is the home page for the Academy of Criminal Justice Sciences, an international organization that promotes scholarly and professional activities in criminal justice.

http://www.asc41.com
This is the home page for the American Society of Criminology, an international organization that promotes research, study, and educational activities in the field of criminology.

http://www.lboro.ac.uk/departments/ss/bsc/homepage/HOMEPAGE.HTM
This is the home page for the British Society of Criminology, the major criminological society of Great Britain. It includes the BSC code of ethics for researchers in the field of criminology.

http://www.sla.purdue.edu/people/soc/mdeflem/zresdes.htm
This site contains an introduction to sociological research methods.

http://arapaho.nsuok.edu/~dreveskr/CJRR.html-ssi
This site contains links to information about research methods and statistics in criminology.

http://personal.tmlp.com/ddemelo/crime/intro.html

This site contains a brief introduction to studying and understanding criminological theory.

PRACTICE QUESTIONS

True/False

_____ 1. Armchair criminologists emphasize the use of research methods.

_____ 2. A hypothesis gains explanatory power from inherent logical consistency.

_____ 3. A researcher who is attempting to evaluate the effectiveness of a new policy is engaged in pure research.

_____ 4. Problem identification often includes statistical analysis.

_____ 5. The task of theory testing predominantly involves rejecting inadequate hypotheses.

_____ 6. A one-group pretest–posttest design eliminates all other possible explanations of behavioral change.

_____ 7. Instrumentation involves the effects of taking a test upon the scores of later testing.

_____ 8. The reactive effects of testing are a threat to external validity.

_____ 9. In a controlled experiment, observable net effects are assumed to be attributable to experimental intervention.

_____ 10. Life histories may only be gathered on single subjects, not on groups of individuals.

_____ 11. Self-report studies are a form of survey research.

_____ 12. Valid experiments can be replicated.

_____ 13. The mode defines the midpoint of a data series.

_____ 14. A statistical test of significance involves testing all members of a given population.

_____ 15. The findings of qualitative methods are expressed numerically.

_____ 16. Informed consent requires that research subjects remain anonymous.

Fill in the Blank

17. One of the criteria for declaring an endeavor scientific is an emphasis on the availability and applicability of the _____.

18. Theories supply _____ within which concepts and variables acquire special significance.

19. An _____ hypothesis is stated in such a way as to facilitate measurement.

20. A threat to _____ validity reduces the researcher's confidence that the intervention will be as effective in the field as under laboratory-like conditions.

21. The problem of _____ occurs when subjects are allowed to decide whether they want to participate in a study.

Chapter 3 Research Methods and Theory Development

22. The use of randomization controls potential threats to _____ validity.

23. _____ involves the analysis of existing data.

24. Mathematical techniques intended to uncover correlations between variables are called_____.

25. When one variable decreases in value as another rises, a _____ correlation exists.

26. Postmodern criminology emphasizes _____ data-gathering strategies.

Multiple Choice

27. _____ is defined as the use of standardized, systematic procedures in the search for knowledge.
    a. A theory
    b. A hypothesis
    c. Research
    d. Geographic profiling

28. The second stage of the research process is to
    a. develop a research design.
    b. review the findings.
    c. choose a data collection technique.
    d. identify a problem.

29. _____ is the process of turning a simple hypothesis into one that is testable.
    a. Theory building
    b. Variable development
    c. Operationalization
    d. Hypothesis testing

30. Given the following research design diagram, what does the "X" stand for?
    $O_1 \ X \ O_2$
    a. The pretest
    b. The posttest
    c. The experimental intervention
    d. None of the above

31. _____ refers to a researcher's ability to generalize research findings to other settings.
    a. Internal validity
    b. Randomization
    c. Confounding effects
    d. External validity

32. The problem of differential selection can be reduced through the use of
    a. statistical regression.
    b. random assignment.
    c. maturation.
    d. experimental mortality.

33. A _____ is especially valuable when aspects of the social setting are beyond the control of the researcher.
    a. controlled experiment
    b. one-group pretest–posttest design
    c. quasi-experimental design
    d. case study

34. Which of the following is not a data-gathering strategy?
    a. Controlled experiment
    b. Participant observation
    c. Life history
    d. Secondary analysis

35. William Foote Whyte's study of Cornerville utilized the _____ strategy.
    a. participant observation
    b. life history
    c. survey
    d. case study

36. The data-gathering technique that does not produce new data is
    a. survey research.
    b. case study.
    c. participant observation.
    d. secondary analysis.

37. _____ statistics attempt to generalize findings by specifying how likely they are to be true for other populations.
    a. Descriptive
    b. Theoretical
    c. Inferential
    d. Hypothetical

38. Adding together all scores and dividing by the total number of observations yields the
    a. mean.
    b. median.
    c. mode.
    d. standard deviation.

39. A _____ correlation exists between sample size and the degree of confidence we can have in our results.
    a. curvilinear
    b. positive
    c. negative
    d. inverse

40. In which of the following areas has research funded by the National Institute of Justice affected social policy?
    a. It has shaped the way that police are deployed.
    b. It has helped to identify career criminals.
    c. It has shown that rehabilitation does not necessarily reduce recidivism.
    d. All of the above

Chapter 3 Research Methods and Theory Development

WORD SEARCH PUZZLE

Case study
Descriptive
Experiment
Hypothesis
Inferential
Qualitative
Quantitative
Randomization

Replicability
Research
Statistics
Survey
Theory
Validity
Variable

```
R A N D O M I Z A T I O N Q E
E E Y S E W C B D H Q C O V S
Y H P L C S Y H K E U C Y C Z
F H X L R I C T Q O A J T S Z
Z T N M I R T R N R N Q I H X
T E N L A C L S I Y T U D Y P
Q H X E K H A Z I P I A I P V
B E S D M X J B W T T L L O Q
N E K H R I F Y I W A I A T N
R E L B A I R A V L T T V H Q
L A I T N E R E F N I A S E D
M M U T G L V P P X V T J S Y
G O Q K W Z U H U X E I Y I R
G T P F J A I A E B E V X S Q
H S U R V D Y D U T S E S A C
```

CROSSWORD PUZZLE

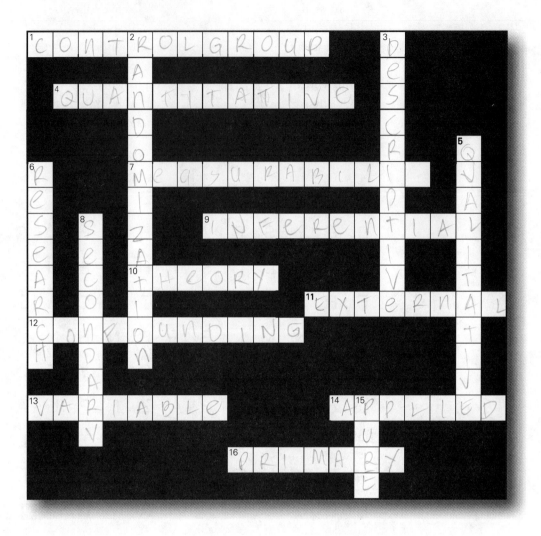

Across

1. Subjects who are not exposed to the experimental intervention. (2 words)
4. _____ methods involve research techniques that produce measurable results.
7. A study of other studies.
9. _____ statistics specify how likely findings are to be true for other populations.
10. A series of interrelated propositions that attempt to describe, explain, predict, and control events.
11. _____ validity is the ability to generalize research findings to other settings.
12. _____ effects are rival explanations or competing hypotheses.
13. A concept that can undergo measurable changes.
14. _____ research is carried out with some practical application in mind.
16. _____ research is characterized by original and direct investigation.

Down

2. The process by which people are assigned to study groups without bias.
3. _____ statistics describe or summarize the relationships within data.
5. _____ methods produce subjective results.
6. The use of standardized, systematic procedures in the search for knowledge.
8. _____ analysis is the reanalysis of preexisting data.
15. _____ research is done for the sake of advancing scientific knowledge.

classical and neoclassical thought

Learning Objectives

After reading this chapter, you should be able to:

1. Recognize the major principles of the Classical School of criminological thought
2. Explain the philosophical bases of classical thought
3. Discuss the Enlightenment, and describe its impact on criminological theorizing
4. Identify modern-day practices that embody principles of the Classical School
5. Discuss the policy implications of the Classical School
6. Assess the shortcomings of the classical approach.

CHAPTER SUMMARY

This chapter introduces the Classical School of criminology, which grew out of concepts and ideas developed by Enlightenment thinkers in the late seventeenth and early eighteenth centuries. It discusses the forerunners of classical thought, including the concepts of morality known as folkways and mores and the method of dividing crimes into the categories of *mala in se* (acts that are fundamentally wrong) and *mala prohibita* (acts that are wrong because they are prohibited). Early sources of the criminal law include the Code of Hammurabi, the Twelve Tables (the basis for early Roman law), English common law, and the Magna Carta, which was eventually expanded into the concept of due process.

The Enlightenment was a social movement that emphasized reason and rational thought. Key intellectual figures included Thomas Hobbes, John Locke, Montesquieu, Jean-Jacques Rousseau, and Thomas Paine. The Enlightenment conceptualized humans as rational beings possessing freedom of choice and led to the development of the Classical School of criminological thought, viewing crime and deviance as products of the exercise of free will. Cesare Beccaria, a key Enlightenment philosopher, published his *Essay on Crimes and Punishments* in 1764, setting forth his philosophy of punishment. Beccaria, who emphasized punishment based on the degree of injury caused, felt that the purpose of punishment should be deterrence (rather than retribution) and saw punishment as a tool to an end (crime prevention) rather than an end in itself. He emphasized the need for adjudication and punishment to be swift and for punishment, once decreed, to be certain. He also felt that punishment should only be severe enough to outweigh the personal benefits to be derived from crime. He opposed the use of torture and accepted the death penalty only for serious crimes against the state.

Jeremy Bentham, another founder of the classical school, developed an approach known as utilitarianism or hedonistic calculus. Bentham believed that humans are rational and weigh the consequences of their behavior, considering pleasure versus pain. Therefore, he emphasized that to prevent crime, the pain of punishment must outweigh the pleasure derived from the crime. Like Beccaria, Bentham considered punishment to be a deterrent for those considering criminal activity.

The classical school emphasized five basic principles, which are fundamental constituents of modern perspectives on crime and human behavior: the principle of rationality, the principle of hedonism, the principle of punishment, the human rights principle, and the due process principle.

By the start of the twentieth century, classical criminology was being replaced by positivism, which rejected the notion of free will and emphasized the concept of hard determinism: the belief that crime results from forces beyond the individual's control. However, by the 1970s, studies suggesting the failure of rehabilitation, combined with an increasing fear of crime, led to a resurgence of classical ideals known as neoclassical criminology.

Rational choice theory was developed out of the neoclassical school of criminology and is based on the belief that criminals make a conscious, rational, and at least partially informed choice to commit crime after weighing the costs and benefits of available alternatives. The two main varieties of choice theory are routine activities theory and situational choice theory. Routine activities theory suggests that crime is likely to occur when a motivated offender and suitable target come together in the absence of a capable guardian and focuses on how lifestyle can contribute to potential victimization. Situational choice theory revolves around the need for criminal opportunity and emphasizes the use of situational crime prevention strategies such as defensible space, improved lighting, and controlling alcohol sales at sporting events. These theories have been criticized for overemphasizing individual choice, disregarding the role of social factors (poverty, poor home environment, inadequate socialization, etc.) on crime causation, and assuming that everyone is equally capable of making rational decisions. Their emphasis on situational crime prevention strategies may also result in displacement rather than true prevention.

Neoclassical thinkers emphasize several purposes of punishment, including retribution, just deserts, and deterrence. Just deserts is the notion that the offender deserves the punishment that he or she receives at the hands of the law. Neoclassical thinkers distinguish between specific and general deterrence. For punishment to be an effective deterrent, it must be swift, certain, and severe enough to outweigh the rewards of the crime. However, these requirements are rarely met by the modern criminal justice system, which may explain the extremely high rates of recidivism in the United States.

The death penalty is probably the most controversial punishment. Research suggests that it may not be an effective general deterrent and that it is applied inequitably. Many capital cases appear to be seriously flawed, resulting in the conviction of innocent individuals. There is also much concern over the disproportionate imposition of the death penalty on racial minorities. There are a large number of arguments both for and against the use of capital punishment in the United States.

There are a number of policy implications to come out of the classical school, including the concepts of determinate sentencing and truth-in-sentencing laws. Current proponents of the classical school are known as law and order advocates and emphasize the need for stiffer laws and enhanced penalties, while arguing against any type of reduction in prison time. Individual rights advocates, on the other hand, emphasize rights over punishment and call for a reduction in the use of imprisonment as a criminal punishment, claiming that the use of incarceration should be determined by the offender's dangerousness and the need for incapacitation.

Overall, the classical and neoclassical schools are more a philosophy of justice than a theory of crime causation. They do not explain how a choice for or against criminal activity is made, nor do they take into account personal motivations. There is no scientific basis for the claims made by the Classical School, and many neoclassical thinkers also emphasize philosophical ideals over scientific research.

KEY CONCEPTS

capable guardian One who effectively discourages crime.

capital punishment The legal imposition of a sentence of death upon a convicted offender. Also called *death penalty*.

Classical School A criminological perspective of the late 1700s and early 1800s that had its roots in the Enlightenment and that held that humans are rational beings, that crime is the result of the exercise of free will, and that punishment can be effective in reducing the incidence of crime, as it negates the pleasure to be derived from crime commission.

Code of Hammurabi An early set of laws established by the Babylonian king Hammurabi, who ruled the ancient city from 1792 to 1750 B.C.

common law Law originating from usage and custom rather than from written statutes. The term refers to nonstatutory customs, traditions, and precedents that help guide judicial decision making.

dangerousness The likelihood that a given individual will later harm society or others. Dangerousness is often measured in terms of recidivism, or the likelihood of new crime commission or rearrest for a new crime within a five-year period following arrest or release from confinement.

determinate sentencing A criminal punishment strategy that mandates a specified and fixed amount of time to be served for every offense category. Under the strategy, for example, all offenders convicted of the same degree of burglary would be sentenced to the same length of time behind bars. Also called *fixed sentencing*.

displacement A shift of criminal activity from one location to another.

Enlightenment A social movement that arose during the eighteenth century and that built upon ideas like empiricism, rationality, free will, humanism, and natural law. Also called *Age of Reason*.

folkways A time-honored custom. Although folkways carry the force of tradition, their violation is unlikely to threaten the survival of the group. See also **more**.

general deterrence A goal of criminal sentencing which seeks to prevent others from committing crimes similar to the one for which a particular offender is being sentenced.

hard determinism The belief that crime results from forces that are beyond the control of the individual.

hedonistic calculus The belief, first proposed by Jeremy Bentham, that behavior holds value to any individual undertaking it according to the amount of pleasure or pain that it can be expected to produce for that person. Also called *utilitarianism*.

incapacitation The use of imprisonment or other means to reduce the likelihood that an offender will be capable of committing future offenses.

individual rights advocates One who seeks to protect personal freedoms in the face of criminal prosecution.

just deserts model The notion that criminal offenders deserve the punishment they receive at the hands of the law and that punishments should be appropriate to the type and severity of crime committed.

law and order advocate One who suggests that under certain circumstances involving criminal threats to public safety, the interests of society should take precedence over individual rights.

mala in se Acts that are thought to be wrong in and of themselves.

mala prohibita Acts that are wrong only because they are prohibited.

mores A behavioral proscription covering potentially serious violations of a group's values. Examples include strictures against murder, rape, and robbery. See also **folkways**.

natural law The philosophical perspective that certain immutable laws are fundamental to human nature and can be readily ascertained through reason. Human-made laws, in contrast, are said to derive from human experience and history-both of which are subject to continual change.

natural rights The rights which, according to natural law theorists, individuals retain in the face of government action and interests.

neoclassical criminology A contemporary version of classical criminology which emphasizes deterrence and retribution, with reduced emphasis on rehabilitation.

nothing-works doctrine The belief, popularized by Robert Martinson in the 1970s, that correctional treatment programs have little success in rehabilitating offenders.

Panopticon A prison designed by Jeremy Bentham which was to be a circular building with cells along the circumference, each clearly visible from a central location staffed by guards.

positivism The application of scientific techniques to the study of crime and criminals.

rational choice theory A perspective which holds that criminality is the result of conscious choice and which predicts that individuals choose to commit crime when the benefits outweigh the costs of disobeying the law.

recidivism The repetition of criminal behavior.

recidivism rate The percentage of convicted offenders who have been released from prison and who are later rearrested for a new crime, generally within five years following release. See also **dangerousness.**

retribution The act of taking revenge upon a criminal perpetrator.

routine activities theory A brand of rational choice theory which suggests that lifestyles contribute significantly to both the volume and type of crime found in any society. Also called *lifestyle theory.*

situational choice theory A brand of rational choice theory which views criminal behavior "as a function of choices and decisions made within a context of situational constraints and opportunities."[1]

situational crime prevention A social policy approach that looks to develop greater understanding of crime and more effective crime prevention strategies through concern with the physical, organizational, and social environments that make crime possible.[2]

social contract The Enlightenment-era concept that human beings abandon their natural state of individual freedom to join together and form society. In the process of forming a social contract, individuals surrender some freedoms to society as a whole, and government, once formed, is obligated to assume responsibilities toward its citizens and to provide for their protection and welfare.

soft determinism The belief that human behavior is the result of choices and decisions made within a context of situational constraints and opportunities.

specific deterrence A goal of criminal sentencing which seeks to prevent a particular offender from engaging in repeat criminality.

target hardening The reduction in criminal opportunity for a particular location, generally through the use of physical barriers, architectural design, and enhanced security measures.

trephination A form of surgery typically involving bone, especially the skull. Early instances of cranial trephination have been taken as evidence for primitive beliefs in spirit possession.

truth in sentencing A close correspondence between the sentence imposed upon those sent to prison and the time actually served prior to prison release.[3]

Twelve Tables Early Roman laws written circa 450 B.C. which regulated family, religious, and economic life.

---

1 Ronald V. Clarke and Derek B. Cornish, eds., *Crime Control in Britain: A Review of Police and Research* (Albany: State University of New York Press), p. 8.
2 David Weisburd, "Reorienting Crime Prevention Research and Policy: From the Causes of Criminality to the Context of Crime," *NIJ Research Report* (Washington, D.C.: National Institute of Justice, June 1997).
3 Lawrence A. Greenfeld, "Prison Sentences and Time Served for Violence," *Bureau of Justice Statistics Selected Findings*, No. 4, April 1995.

CHAPTER OUTLINE

I. Introduction

II. Major Principles of the Classical School

III. Forerunners of Classical Thought

    A. The Demonic Era

    B. Early Sources of the Criminal Law

    C. The Enlightenment

IV. The Classical School

    A. Cesare Beccaria (1738-1794)

    B. Jeremy Bentham (1748-1832)

    C. Heritage of the Classical School

V. Neoclassical Criminology

    A. Rational Choice Theory

    B. The Seductions of Crime

    C. Situational Crime Control Policy

    D. Critique of Rational Choice Theory

VI. Punishment and Neoclassical Thought

    A. Just Deserts

    B. Deterrence

Chapter 4 Classical and Neoclassical Thought

        C. The Death Penalty _____

  VII. Policy Implications of the Classical School _____

        A. Law and Order versus Individual Rights _____

 VIII. A Critique of Classical Theories _____

DISCUSSION QUESTIONS

These discussion questions are found in the textbook at the end of the chapter. Your instructor may want to focus on these questions at the conclusion of the lecture on Chapter 4.

1. This book emphasizes a social problems versus social responsibility theme. Which perspective is most clearly supported by classical and neoclassical thought? Why?

2. Name the various preclassical thinkers identified in this chapter. What ideas did each contribute to Enlightenment philosophy? What form did those ideas take in classical criminological thought?

3. Define *natural law*. Do you believe that natural law exists? If so, what types of behaviors would be contravened by natural law? If not, why not?

4. What is meant by the idea of a "social contract"? How does the concept of social contract relate to natural law?

5. What were the central concepts that defined the Classical School of criminological thought? Which of those concepts are still alive? Where do you see evidence for the survival of those concepts?

6. What are the major differences between individual rights advocates and law and order advocates? Which perspective most appeals to you? Why? Which is most closely aligned with classical criminology?

7. Define *recidivism*. What is a recidivism rate? Why are recidivism rates so high today? What can be done to lower them?

STUDENT EXERCISES

Activity 1

Your instructor will place you in groups and assign you to a public venue (a library, a grocery store, a video store, an office building, etc.) Your group is to inspect the location and answer the following questions:

1. What situational crime prevention techniques are in use in this location? What types of crime do they attempt to prevent? (For example, metal detectors to help prevent the theft of library books)

2. What additional techniques might be employed to reduce crime in this location?

Activity 2

Your instructor will divide the class into groups. Each group is to read the U.S. Constitution (including the Bill of Rights) and prepare a short report on how this document was influenced by the principles of the classical school of criminology, including specific examples.

Activity 3

Your instructor will provide you with a list of the UCR Part II offenses and ask you to classify each offense as either a *mala in se* or *mala prohibita* crime. You will then be placed into groups. Within each group, compare and contrast their classifications and determine where there is disagreement. Focus on the wide range of opinions present among a fairly homogeneous group (criminal justice majors at a university) and discuss possible reasons for these differing opinions.

CRIMINOLOGY TODAY ON THE WEB

http://www.crimetheory.com/Archive/Beccaria/index.html
This site contains the text of Cesare Beccaria's essay *On Crimes and Punishment*.

http://www.deathpenaltyinfo.org
This is the Web site for the Death Penalty Information Center, a nonprofit organization which provides the public with information on a variety of topics related to the issue of capital punishment.

Chapter 4 Classical and Neoclassical Thought

http://www.yale.edu/lawweb/avalon/avalon.htm

This is the Web site for Yale University's Avalon Project. It includes the text of many legal and historical documents, including the Code of Hammurabi and the Magna Carta.

http://is.gseis.ucla.edu/impact/f96/Projects/dengberg

This site contains a virtual Panopticon.

PRACTICE QUESTIONS

True/False

_____ 1. Rape is a *mala in se* crime.

_____ 2. The Magna Carta was signed by King Edward the Confessor.

_____ 3. John Locke focused primarily on the responsibilities of individuals to the societies of which they are a part.

_____ 4. Natural rights are inherent in the social contract between citizens and their government.

_____ 5. Beccaria saw punishment as an end in itself.

_____ 6. Beccaria considered a jury of one's peers to be useless.

_____ 7. Probation and victim restitution fall into Bentham's concept of compulsive punishment.

_____ 8. Soft determinism suggests that crime results from forces beyond the control of the individual.

_____ 9. Routine activities theory is an extension of the rational choice perspective.

_____ 10. According to Jack Katz, crime may be sensually compelling to the offender.

_____ 11. Rational choice theory assumes that not everyone is capable of making rational decisions.

_____ 12. High recidivism rates suggest that criminal punishments do not effectively deter crime.

_____ 13. Advocates of determinate sentencing believe that the fixed amount of punishment necessary for deterrence can be calculated and specified.

_____ 14. Individual rights advocates call for an increase in the use of imprisonment as a criminal sanction.

Fill in the Blank

15. Criminal homicide is a *mala* _____ crime.

16. The _____ is one of the first known bodies of law to survive to the present day.

17. Common law was declared the law of the land in England by King _____.

18. The concept of _____ suggests that certain immutable laws are fundamental to human nature and can be ascertained through reason.

19. According to Beccaria, oaths were _____ in a court of law.

20. _____ theory uses cost-benefit analysis.

21. Property identification falls into the _____ category of situational crime control.

22. The _____ model of criminal sentencing involves the belief that criminal offenders deserve their punishment.

23. _____ requires judges to assess and make public the actual time an offender is likely to serve once sentenced to prison.

Multiple Choice

24. _____ are time-honored customs which are preferred but which do not threaten the survival of the social group if they are violated.
    a. Mores
    b. Folkways
    c. Laws
    d. Crimes

25. Which of the following is not a *mala prohibita* crime?
    a. gambling
    b. premarital sexual behavior
    c. drug use
    d. theft

26. Which of the following was not one of the legal documents contained in the Justinian Code?
    a. The Summary
    b. The Institutes
    c. The Digest
    d. The Code

27. Which of the following was not a significant Enlightenment thinker?
    a. Thomas Hobbes
    b. John Locke
    c. Francis Bacon
    d. William Sumner

28. _____ is a concept which suggests that certain immutable laws are fundamental to human nature and can be ascertained through reason.
    a. Natural law
    b. Natural rights
    c. Positive law
    d. Hedonistic calculus

29. Which of the following was not one of the three types of crimes outlined by Beccaria?
    a. Crimes that ran contrary to the social order
    b. Crimes that threatened the security of the state
    c. Crimes that injured citizens or their property
    d. Crimes that involved no victims other than society

30. According to Bentham, _____ punishment includes starvation and whipping.
    a. capital
    b. restrictive
    c. chronic
    d. afflictive

31. The Panopticon was designed by
    a. Beccaria.
    b. Sumner.
    c. Locke.
    d. Bentham.

32. The "nothing works" concept was based on the work of
    a. James Q. Wilson.
    b. David Fogel.
    c. Robert Martinson.
    d. Lawrence Cohen.

33. The situational choice perspective was developed by
    a. Larry Cohen and Marcus Felson.
    b. Hal Pepinsky and Richard Quinney.
    c. Ronald Clarke and Derek Cornish.
    d. Walter DeKeseredy and Jock Young.

34. Rational choice theory emphasizes primarily
    a. pleasure and pain.
    b. emotionality.
    c. rationality and cognition.
    d. none of the above

35. _____ sees the primary utility of punishment as revenge.
    a. Deterrence
    b. Retribution
    c. Rehabilitation
    d. Incapacitation

36. According to advocates of general deterrence, which of the following is not required for punishment to be an effective impediment to crime?
    a. The punishment must be harsh.
    b. The punishment must be swift.
    c. The punishment must be severe.
    d. The punishment must be certain.

37. In 2000, the governor of _____ suspended all executions in the state.
    a. Texas
    b. Illinois
    c. Georgia
    d. Florida

38. _____ advocates emphasize individual responsibility and hold offenders responsible for their actions.
    a. Law and order
    b. Common law
    c. Individual rights
    d. Natural law

39. The use of imprisonment or other means to reduce the likelihood that an offender will be capable of committing future crimes is known as
    a. deterrence.
    b. retribution.
    c. rehabilitation.
    d. incapacitation.

40. _____ advocates emphasize rights over punishment.
    a. Law and order
    b. Common law
    c. Individual rights
    d. Natural rights

WORD SEARCH PUZZLE

Classical
Dangerousness
Determinism
Deterrence
Displacement
Folkways
Incapacitation
Mores

Neoclassical
Panopticon
Positivism
Recidivism
Retribution
Trephination
Utilitarianism

```
N Q R N N K O V E Z M M F N D
D O V M O R V G S S N S O U E
U T I L I T A R I A N I S M T
R F W T T O S V C N T N S N E
X L X H A H I V O U P I E Z R
K U S X N T Y C B J W N N P R
I L E D I U I I N D E R S U E
F D R S H T R C F C B E U R N
I L O J P T B D A L N T O C C
M P M O E N W L D P I E R Z E
L G N R R U P J O N A D E I P
H A N E T S F H J M U C G E A
P L A C I S S A O C O E N W I
M A Z D S Y A W K L O F A I Q
M S I V I D I C E R F D D U K
```

Chapter 4 Classical and Neoclassical Thought

CROSSWORD PUZZLE

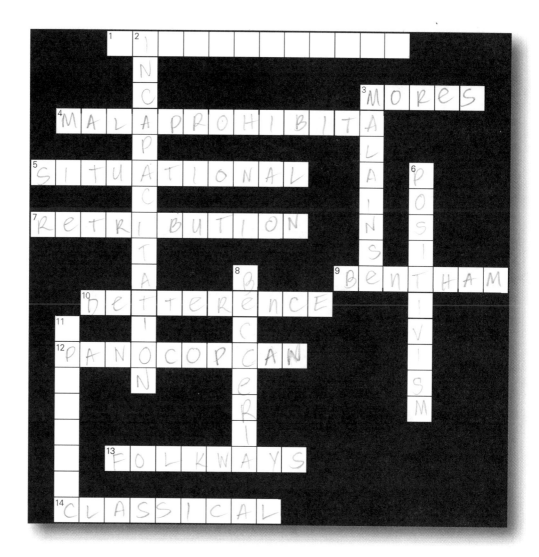

Across

1. A shift of criminal activity from one spatial location to another.
3. Behavioral proscriptions covering potentially serious violations of group values.
4. Acts that are wrong because they are forbidden. (2 words)
5. _____ crime prevention focuses on the environment that makes crime possible
7. Taking revenge against a criminal perpetrator.
9. The developer of the hedonistic calculus approach.
10. The prevention of crime.
12. Jeremy Bentham's prison design.
13. Time-honored customs carrying the force of tradition.
14. The _____ school suggests that humans are rational.

Down

2. The use of imprisonment to reduce an offender's ability to commit future crimes.
3. Acts thought to be wrong in and of themselves. (3 words)
6. A study of crime based on determinism.
8. Author of *Essay on Crimes and Punishments*.
11. The type of deterrence which prevents a particular individual from recidivating.

biological roots of criminal behavior

CHAPTER 5

Learning Objectives

After reading this chapter, you should be able to:

1. Recognize the importance of biological explanations of criminal behavior
2. Identify the fundamental assumptions made by biological theorists of crime causation
3. Explain the relationship between human aggression and biological determinants
4. Describe the research linking genetics and crime
5. Explain the contribution of sociobiology to the study of criminality
6. Identify modern-day social policies that reflects the biological approach to crime causation
7. Assess the shortcomings of biological theories of criminal behavior

CHAPTER SUMMARY

This chapter introduces biological theories of human behavior; an area that generates a considerable amount of skepticism and controversy among criminologists. Many early biological theories fall into the category of criminal anthropology: the scientific study of the relationship between human physical characteristics and criminality. These include physiognomy, a theory with roots in ancient Greece, and phrenology, developed by Franz Joseph Gall. One of the best-known early positivists was Cesare Lombroso, who developed the theory of atavism, suggesting that most offenders are born criminals. He also identified other categories of offenders, including criminaloids, or occasional criminals, insane criminals, and criminals incited by passion. A number of later researchers evaluated atavism; Charles Goring found no support for the theory, and Earnest Hooton concluded that criminals were physiologically inferior.

Constitutional theories examine body types. One of the best known constitutional theories is somatotyping, a theory associated with Ernest Kretschmer and William H. Sheldon. Sheldon identified four main body types, linked them to personality, and concluded that the mesomorph was most likely to be associated with criminality and delinquency.

Researchers have also linked criminal behavior to factors such as sugar or coffee consumption, food allergies, food additives, and vitamins, although the role of food and diet in producing criminal behavior has not been well established. Environmental pollution of lead, manganese, and other toxic metals also has been linked to violent crime. Prenatal exposure to substances such as tobacco smoke, alcohol, and marijuana have been found to be related to various behavioral factors, including delinquency. Various hormones, such as testosterone, serotonin, and cortisol, have been shown to be associated with aggression. Temperature has also been shown to have an influence on both violent and property crime, although it is moderated by temporal factors such as the time of day and day of the week.

Research into criminal families, such as the Jukes and the Kallikaks, led to the development of eugenic criminology and the eugenics movement of the late 1920s and early 1930s; this has been largely discredited. Research into the XYY or "supermale" has also concluded that XYY males are not predictably aggressive. More recently, Dutch criminologists may have identified a specific gene with links to criminal behavior. The use of twins to study genetic influences have found support for a substantial influence of heredity on delinquent and criminal behavior. The Human Genome Project may eventually help to uncover more information about the role of genetics in criminality. Gender differences in criminal behavior have remained extremely regular over time, refuting claims of criminologists such as Freda Adler, who suggest that cultural changes producing increased opportunity for female criminality would lead to an increase in crimes by women. Edward O. Wilson's paradigm of sociobiology involves systematic study of the biological basis of social behavior and emphasizes altruism and territoriality as determinants of behavior. Sociobiology has garnered considerable criticism as well as increased recognition.

A recent synthesis of biological and environmental factors was presented by James Q. Wilson and Richard Herrnstein in their book *Crime and Human Nature*. They identify a number of constitutional factors, such as age, gender, body type, intelligence, and personality, as contributing to crime.

The impact of biological theories on public policy has led to considerable controversy. Some fear issues such as racial prejudice or the resurgence of a new eugenics movement. In addition, contemporary criminologists have provided focused critiques of biological perspectives on crime, including methodological and other concerns. It does appear that various biological factors are correlated with various measures of criminal behavior, although the influence of social factors has overshadowed the relationship.

KEY CONCEPTS

atavism A term used by Cesare Lombroso to suggest that criminals are physiological throwbacks to earlier stages of human evolution. The term is derived from the Latin term *atavus*, which means "ancestor."

behavioral genetics The study of genetic and environmental contributions to individual variations in human behavior.

biological theory (of criminology) A theory that maintains that the basic determinants of human behavior, including criminality, are constitutionally or physiologically based and often inherited.

born criminal An individual who is born with a genetic predilection toward criminality.

constitutional theory A theory that explains criminality by reference to offenders' body types, inheritance, genetics, or external observable physical characteristics.

criminal anthropology The scientific study of the relationship between human physical characteristics and criminality.

criminaloids A term used by Cesare Lombroso to describe occasional criminals who were pulled into criminality primarily by environmental influences.

cycloid A term developed by Ernst Kretschmer to describe a particular relationship between body build and personality type. The cycloid personality, which was associated with a heavy-set, soft type of body, was said to vacillate between normality and abnormality.

ectomorph A body type originally described as thin and fragile, with long, slender, poorly muscled extremities and delicate bones.

endomorph A body type originally described as soft and round or overweight.

eugenic criminology A perspective which holds that the root causes of criminality are passed from generation to generation in the form of "bad genes."

eugenics The study of hereditary improvement by genetic control.

genetic determinism The belief that genes are the major determining factor in human behavior.

hypoglycemia A medical condition characterized by low blood sugar.

Juke family A well-known "criminal family" studied by Richard L. Dugdale.

Kallikak family A well-known "criminal family" studied by Henry H. Goddard.

masculinity hypothesis A belief (from the late 1800s), that criminal women typically exhibited masculine features and mannerisms. In the late 1900s, the belief that, over time, men and women will commit crimes that are increasingly similar in nature, seriousness and frequency. Increasing similarity in crime commission is predicted to result from changes in the social status of women (for example, better economic position, gender role convergence, socialization practices that are increasingly similar for both males and females, and so on).

mesomorph A body type described as athletic and muscular.

monozygotic (MZ) twins Twins that develop from the same egg and that carry virtually the same genetic material.

paradigm An example, model, or theory.

phrenology The study of the shape of the head to determine anatomical correlates of human behavior.

sociobiology "The systematic study of the biological basis of all social behavior."[1]

somatotyping The classification of human beings into types according to body build and other physical characteristics.

supermale A male individual displaying the XYY chromosome structure.

testosterone The primary male sex hormone. Produced in the testes, its function is to control secondary sex characteristics and sexual drive.

CHAPTER OUTLINE

I. Introduction _____
_____

II. Major Principles of Biological Theories _____
_____

III. Biological Roots of Human Aggression _____
_____

    A. Early Biological Theories _____
_____

    B. Body Types _____
_____

    C. Chemical and Environmental Precursors of Crime _____
_____

    D. Hormones and Criminality _____
_____

    E. Weather and Crime _____
_____

IV. Genetics and Crime _____
_____

    A. Criminal Families _____
_____

    B. The XYY "Supermale" _____
_____

    C. Chromosomes and Modern-Day Criminal Families _____
_____

    D. Behavioral Genetics _____
_____

    E. The Human Genome Project _____
_____

---

1 Edward O. Wilson, *Sociobiology: The New Synthesis* (Cambridge: Harvard University Press, Belknap Press, 1975).

Chapter 5 Biological Roots of Criminal Behavior

    F. Male-Female Differences in Criminality _____

    G. Sociobiology _____

  V. Crime and Human Nature: A Contemporary Synthesis _____

 VI. Policy Issues _____

VII. Critiques of Biological Theories _____

DISCUSSION QUESTIONS

These discussion questions are found in the textbook at the end of the chapter. Your instructor may want to focus on these questions at the conclusion of the lecture on Chapter 5.

1. This book emphasizes a social problems versus social responsibility theme. Which perspective is best supported by biological theories of crime causation? Why?

2. What are the central features of biological theories of crime? How do such theories differ from other perspectives that attempt to explain the same phenomena?

3. Why have biological approaches to crime causation been out of vogue lately? Do you agree or disagree with those who are critical of such perspectives? Why?

4. What does the author of this book mean when he writes, "[o]pen inquiry…requires objective consideration of all points of view and an unbiased examination of each for its ability to shed light on the subject under study"? Do you agree or disagree with this assertion? Why?

5. What are the social policy implications of biological theories of crime? What U.S. Supreme Court case, discussed in this chapter, might presage a type of policy based on such theories?

STUDENT EXERCISES

Activity 1

Watch several episodes of a reality-based television show such as *Cops*. Observe the suspects in each crime/event and record as much information as possible about their physical characteristics. Do you notice any common physical characteristics among the suspects? Does there appear to be a "criminal type"?

In addition, watch several episodes of a non-reality-based show and record information about the physical characteristics of the actors playing the criminals. Do fictional television shows cast actors of a certain physical type to play offenders? What characteristics (if any) are common to fictional criminals?

Activity 2

Review the elements that C. Ray Jeffrey states should be included in a comprehensive biologically based program of crime prevention and control. Discuss the ethical implications of these components.

Activity 3

In your university library, obtain information on Youth Violence Initiative, a program proposed during the Bush administration in the early 1990s. Do you think that this program should have been canceled by President Clinton? Why or why not?

CRIMINOLOGY TODAY ON THE WEB

http://www.epub.org.br/cm/n01/frenolog/frenologia.htm
This Web site makes available an article about phrenology and the theory behind it.

http://www.crimetheory.com/Archive/BvB/index.html
This Web site includes the U.S. Supreme Court's 1927 ruling in the case *Buck v. Bell*.

http://www.ornl.gov/TechResources/Human_Genome
This is the home page of the Human Genome Project.

http://www.crime-times.org
This is the Web site of *Crime Times,* a national newsletter reporting on research conducted in the area of biological causes of crime.

Chapter 5 Biological Roots of Criminal Behavior

PRACTICE QUESTIONS

True/False

_____ 1. A fundamental assumption of biological theories is that some humans may be further along the evolutionary ladder than others.

_____ 2. The theory of phrenology was developed by Konrad Lorenz.

_____ 3. Cesare Lombroso was a positivist.

_____ 4. Positivism emphasizes observation and measurement.

_____ 5. Criminoloids do not exhibit atavism.

_____ 6. Earnest Hooton favored the development of rehabilitation programs.

_____ 7. Ernst Kretschmer's cycloid personality was associated with an athletic and muscular body.

_____ 8. Recent research published in the *New England Journal of Medicine* confirms the belief that diets high in sugar may lead to hyperactivity.

_____ 9. Research has found a significant correlation between juvenile crime and high levels of lead.

_____ 10. PMS as a defense has been accepted by the courts.

_____ 11. Weather has no significant influence on human behavior.

_____ 12. Goddard concluded that criminality was inherited.

_____ 13. The XYY defense has never been used successfully in court.

_____ 14. If human behavior has a substantial heritable component, any observed relationship might be expected to be stronger between monozygotic than between dizygotic twins.

_____ 15. Current research finds clear support for Freda Adler's theory that a new female criminal is emerging.

_____ 16. According to Ellis and Walsh, there are probably no genes for criminal behavior.

Fill in the Blank

17. Biological theories of crime causation assume that the basic determinants of behavior are _____ based.

18. Phrenology is also known as _____.

19. Positivism emphasizes the application of _____ to the study of crime.

20. _____ conducted a study of Lombroso's theory and concluded that criminals show an overall physiological inferiority to the general population.

21. According to Ernst Kretschmer, _____ committed primarily nonviolent property crimes.

22. Sheldon and Eleanor Glueck associated mesomorphy with _____.

23. Research suggests that _____ brain levels of serotonin might reduce aggression.

24. More _____ crime is reported to the police on warm than on cold days.

25. Research has found a _____ correlation between temperature and violent crime.

26. The eugenics movement policies were endorsed by the U.S. Supreme Court in the case of _____.

27. Identical twins are known as _____ twins.

28. According to Wilson and Herrnstein, criminality is consistently associated with _____ intelligence.

Multiple Choice

29. Which of the following is not one of the fundamental assumptions of biological theories of crime causation?
    a. The brain is the organ of behavior.
    b. The basic determinants of criminal behavior are, to a considerable degree, the product of individual choice.
    c. A tendency to commit crime may be inherited.
    d. They are all fundamental assumptions of biological theories.

30. The early biological theory which studied the shape of the head to predict criminality was known as
    a. atavism.
    b. physiognomy.
    c. somatotyping.
    d. phrenology.

31. _____ is a concept used by Cesare Lombroso to suggest that criminality is the result of primitive urges which survived the evolutionary process.
    a. Ectomorph
    b. Atavism
    c. Schizoid
    d. Criminaloid

32. Which of the following traits is especially characteristic of a murderer, according to Lombroso?
    a. A diseased personality
    b. A nonstandard number of ribs
    c. A large amount of body hair
    d. Cold glassy eyes

33. _____ reported finding physiological features characteristic of specific criminal types in individual states.
    a. Cesare Lombroso
    b. Earnest Hooton
    c. Charles Goring
    d. William Sheldon

34. Which of the following was not one of Ernst Kretschmer's mental categories?
    a. Schizoids
    b. Criminaloids
    c. Cycloids
    d. Displastics

Chapter 5 Biological Roots of Criminal Behavior

35. Which of the following foods has not been implicated in the production of criminal violence?
    a. Coffee
    b. MSG
    c. Processed foods
    d. All of the above may possibly trigger antisocial behavior.

36. The relationship between testosterone and aggressive behavior in young males appears to be moderated by
    a. age.
    b. the social environment.
    c. genetics.
    d. none of the above

37. According to Cohn and Rotton, the relationship between temperature and assaults is strongest during the _____ hours.
    a. evening
    b. morning
    c. afternoon
    d. midday

38. The studies of the Jukes and Kallikak families emphasized _____ as the primary source of criminality.
    a. environment
    b. ecology
    c. genetics
    d. psychology

39. The purpose of the Human Genome Project is to determine the complete sequence of
    a. DNA.
    b. RNA.
    c. XYY.
    d. MAOA.

40. According to sociobiologists, the violence and aggressiveness associated with territoriality is often reserved for
    a. family members.
    b. relatives.
    c. acquaintances.
    d. strangers.

WORD SEARCH PUZZLE

Atavism
Criminaloids
Cycloid
Ectomorph
Endomorph
Eugenics
Heritability
Hypoglycemia
Kallikak
Mesomorph
Paradigm
Phrenology
Sociobiology
Somatotyping
Testosterone

```
C R I M I N A L O I D S N D Z
Y P A R A D I G M S I V A T A
G T G D W E N D O M O R P H P
O V I H M M E S O M O R P H R
L K A L L I K A K H R R D Z N
O S O C I O B I O L O G Y J E
N K W H P B A F K M P I N W U
E M Q S O M A T O T Y P I N G
R V E N O R E T S O T S E T E
H J A P R S C D I O L C Y C N
P B Q R V E V B D R X V G F I
T Z H Y P O G L Y C E M I A C
D R X J A M U M X W R H W O S
```

Chapter 5 Biological Roots of Criminal Behavior

CROSSWORD PUZZLE

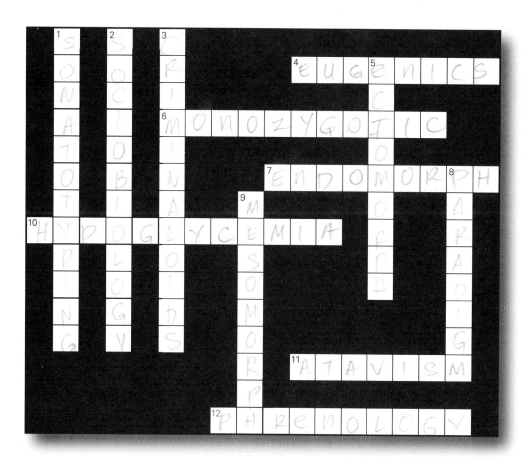

Across

4. The study of hereditary improvement by genetic control
6. Twins that developed from the same egg.
7. A body type that is soft and round.
10. A condition characterized by low blood sugar.
11. Lombroso's concept that criminals are physiological throwbacks.
12. Studying the shape of the head for correlates of human behavior.

Down

1. Classifying humans according to body build.
2. The systematic study of the biological basis of social behavior.
3. Lombroso's term to describe occasional criminals pulled into crime by environmental influences.
5. A body type that is thin and fragile.
8. An example, model, or theory.
9. A body type that is athletic and muscular.

psychological and psychiatric foundations of criminal behavior

Learning Objectives

After reading this chapter, you should be able to:

1. Identify the contributions of psychology and psychiatry to the understanding of criminal behavior
2. Explain the relationship between personality and criminal behavior
3. Recognize the importance of modeling theory to an understanding of criminality
4. Understand the unique characteristics of those found not guilty by reason of insanity
5. Identify current social policy that reflects the psychological approach to criminal behavior

CHAPTER SUMMARY

This chapter introduces psychological and psychiatric theories of human behavior. Most early psychological theories emphasized either behavioral conditioning or personality disturbances and psychopathology. The concept of the psychopath or sociopath was developed by Hervey Cleckley. Currently, these terms have fallen out of favor and have been replaced by the concept of antisocial personality. Individuals with the characteristics of an antisocial personality are likely to become criminals at some point. Another theory emphasizing personality characteristics is biopsychology, which was developed by Hans Eysenck. Eysenck described three personality dimensions (psychoticism, extroversion, and neuroticism), each with links to criminality. He stated that personality traits were dependent on the autonomic nervous system; those whose nervous systems require stimulation are more likely to become offenders.

Sigmund Freud's psychoanalytic theory suggests that criminal behavior is maladaptive, the result of inadequacies inherent in the offender's personality. Psychoanalysis suggests that one possible cause of crime may be a poorly developed superego, which leaves the individual operating without a moral guide. Neurosis, a minor form of mental illness, may also lead to crime. In addition, more serious mental illness such as psychosis may result in criminal behavior, including violent crime. Freud's frustration aggression link was more fully developed by researchers such as J. Dollard, who suggested that everyone suffers frustration, and thus aggression is a natural part of life; it may be manifested in socially acceptable or unacceptable ways. Other theorists suggest that crime fulfills some purpose, such as the need to be punished or the need to reduce stress.

Modeling theory, as developed by Albert Bandura, is a form of social learning theory that suggests that people learn to act by observing others; observation of aggressive behavior teaches one how to behave aggressively. Behavior theory, developed by researchers such as B.F. Skinner, involves the use of rewards and punishments to control a person's responses, or operant behavior. Attachment theory suggests that the lack of a secure attachment between a child and his/her primary caregiver may lead to delinquent and criminal behavior later in life. Michael Gottfredson and Travis Hirschi developed a general theory of crime based on the concept that low self-control accounts for all types of crime.

Insanity is a legal rather than a clinical concept and is based on the claim of mental illness. Insanity is a defense to criminal prosecution and the burden of proof is on the defendant; a person is presumed sane at the start of a criminal trial. The 1984 federal Insanity Defense Reform Act (IDRA) created the verdict of not guilty by reason of insanity (NGRI), ensured that a federal defendant found NGRI will be hospitalized rather than released, and included a provision permitting mentally ill persons to be held for trial in the hopes that they will recover sufficiently to permit the trial to proceed. Several tests for insanity are used in the United States. The *M'Naughten* rule holds that people cannot be held criminally responsible for their actions if at the time of the crime they either did not know what they were doing or did not know that what they were doing is wrong. The irresistible-impulse test, which can be used alone or in conjunction with *M'Naughten*, holds that people are not guilty of criminal offenses if by virtue of their mental state or psychological condition, they were unable to resist committing the criminal act. Other tests include the *Durham* rule, the substantial-capacity test, and the *Brawner* rule. Some states permit verdicts of guilty but mentally ill (GBMI), which allows the defendant to be held responsible for a crime despite the presence of some degree of mental incompetence.

The use of psychological theories to predict or assess dangerousness has contributed to social policy. The concept of selective incapacitation is based on the notion of career criminals and relies on prediction of future criminality to determine sentencing policy. Correctional psychology is concerned with the diagnosis and classification of offenders, the treatment of correctional populations, and the rehabilitation of offenders. Psychological profiling is used to help police better understand people wanted for serious crimes.

Chapter 6 Psychological and Psychiatric Foundations of Criminal Behavior

KEY CONCEPTS

alloplastic adaptation A form of adjustment which results from changes in the environment surrounding an individual.

antisocial personality A term used to describe individuals who are basically unsocialized and whose behavior pattern brings them repeatedly into conflict with society. Also called *asocial personality*.

antisocial personality disorder A psychological condition exhibited by "individuals who are basically unsocialized and whose behavior pattern brings them repeatedly into conflicts with society."[1]

attachment theory A social-psychological perspective on delinquent and criminal behavior which holds that the successful development of secure attachment between a child and his or her primary caregiver provides the basic foundation for all future psychological development.

autoplastic adaptation A form of adjustment which results from changes within an individual.

behavior theory A psychological perspective which posits that individual behavior which is rewarded will increase in frequency, while that which is punished will decrease.

Brawner **rule** A somewhat vague rule for determining insanity that was created in the federal court case of *U.S. v. Brawner* (471 F.2d 969) and in which the jury is asked to decide whether the defendant could be *justly* held responsible for the criminal act with which he or she stands charged, in the face of any claims of insanity or mental incapacity.

conditioning A psychological principle which holds that the frequency of any behavior can be increased or decreased through reward, punishment, or association with other stimuli.

correctional psychology The branch of forensic psychology concerned with the diagnosis and classification of offenders, the treatment of correctional populations, and the rehabilitation of inmates and other law violators.

Durham **rule** A standard for judging legal insanity which holds that an accused is not criminally responsible if his unlawful act was the product of mental disease or mental defect.

ego The reality-testing part of the personality. Also called the *reality principle*. More formally, the personality component that is conscious, most immediately controls behavior, and is most in touch with external reality.[2]

electroencephalogram (EEG) The electrical measurement of brain wave activity.

forensic psychiatry A branch of psychiatry having to do with the study of crime and criminality.

forensic psychology The application of the science and profession of psychology to questions and issues relating to law and the legal system.[3]

frustration-aggression theory A theory that holds that frustration, which is a natural consequence of living, is a root cause of crime. Criminal behavior can be a form of adaptation when it results in stress reduction.

---

[1] American Board of Forensic Psychology, World Wide Web site. Web posted at http://www.abfp.com/brochure.html. Accessed November 22, 2000.
[2] *American Heritage Dictionary and Electronic Thesaurus* (Boston: Houghton Mifflin, 1987).
[3] American Board of Forensic Psychology, World Wide Web site. Web posted at http://www.abfp.com/brochure.html. Accessed November 22, 2000.

guilty but mentally ill (GBMI) A finding that offenders are guilty of the criminal offense with which they are charged, but because of their prevailing mental condition, they are generally sent to psychiatric hospitals for treatment rather than to prison. Once they have been declared cured, however, such offenders can be transferred to correctional facilities to serve out their sentences.

id The aspect of the personality from which drives, wishes, urges, and desires emanate. More formally, the division of the psyche associated with instinctual impulses and demands for immediate satisfaction of primitive needs.[4]

insanity (legal) A legally established inability to understand right from wrong or to conform one's behavior to the requirements of the law.

insanity (psychological) Persistent mental disorder or derangement.[5]

irresistible-impulse test A standard for judging legal insanity which holds that a defendant is not guilty of a criminal offense if the person, by virtue of his or her mental state or psychological condition, was not able to resist committing the crime.

***M'Naughten* rule** A standard for judging legal insanity which requires that offenders not know what they were doing, or if they did, that they not know it was wrong.

modeling theory A form of social learning theory which asserts that people learn how to act by observing others.

neurosis Functional disorders of the mind or of the emotions involving anxiety, phobia, or other abnormal behavior.

operant behavior Behavior that affects the environment in such a way as to produce responses or further behavioral cues.

paranoid schizophrenics A schizophrenic individual who suffers from delusions and hallucinations.

psychiatric criminology Theories derived from the medical sciences, including neurology, and which, like other psychological theories, focus on the individual as the unit of analysis. Psychiatric theories form the basis of psychiatric criminology. See also **forensic psychiatry**.

psychiatric theory A theory derived from the medical sciences, including neurology, and which, like other psychological theories, focuses on the individual as the unit of analysis.

psychoanalysis The theory of human psychology founded by Sigmund Freud on the concepts of the unconscious, resistance, repression, sexuality, and the Oedipus complex.[6]

psychoanalytic criminology A psychiatric approach developed by Sigmund Freud which emphasizes the role of personality in human behavior and which sees deviant behavior as the result of dysfunctional personalities.

psychological profiling The attempt to categorize, understand, and predict the behavior of certain types of offenders based on behavioral clues they provide.

psychological theory A theory derived from the behavioral sciences which focuses on the individual as the unit of analysis. Psychological theories place the locus of crime causation within the personality of the individual offender.

---

4 Ibid.
5 Ibid.
6 *American Heritage Dictionary and Electronic Thesaurus.*

Chapter 6 Psychological and Psychiatric Foundations of Criminal Behavior

psychopath An individual with a personality disorder, especially one manifested in aggressively antisocial behavior, which is often said to be the result of a poorly developed superego. Also called *sociopath*.

psychopathology The study of pathological mental conditions-that is, mental illness.

psychosis A form of mental illness in which sufferers are said to be out of touch with reality.

psychotherapy A form of psychiatric treatment based on psychoanalytical principles and techniques.

punishment An undesirable behavioral consequence likely to decrease the frequency of occurrence of that behavior.

reward A desirable behavioral consequence likely to increase the frequency of occurrence of that behavior.

schizoid A person characterized by schizoid personality disorder. Such disordered personalities appear to be aloof, withdrawn, unresponsive, humorless, dull and solitary to an abnormal degree.

schizophrenic A mentally ill individual who is out of touch with reality and who suffers from disjointed thinking.

selective incapacitation A social policy which seeks to protect society by incarcerating the individuals deemed to be the most dangerous.

self-control A person's ability to alter his or her own states and responses.[7]

sublimation The psychological process whereby one aspect of consciousness comes to be symbolically substituted for another.

substantial-capacity test A standard for judging legal insanity which requires that a person lack the mental capacity needed to understand the wrongfulness of his act, or to conform his behavior to the requirements of the law.

superego The moral aspect of the personality; much like the conscience. More formally, the division of the psyche that develops by the incorporation of the perceived moral standards of the community, is mainly unconscious, and includes the conscience.[8]

thanatos A death wish.

total institution A facility from which individuals can rarely come and go and in which communal life is intense and circumscribed. Individuals in total institutions tend to eat, sleep, play, learn, and worship (if at all) together.

CHAPTER OUTLINE

I. Introduction _____
_____

II. Major Principles of Psychological Theories _____
_____

---

[7] Roy F Baumeister and Julie Juola Exline, "Self-control, Morality, and Human Strength," *Journal of Social & Clinical Psychology*, Vol. 19, No. 1 (April 2000), p. 29-42.
[8] *American Heritage Dictionary and Electronic Thesaurus*.

III. Early Psychological Theories _____

    A. The Psychopath _____

    B. Antisocial Personality Disorder _____

    C. Personality Types and Crime _____

    D. Early Psychiatric Theories _____

IV. Criminal Behavior as Maladaption _____

    A. The Psychoanalytic Perspective _____

    B. The Psychotic Offender _____

    C. The Link between Frustration and Aggression _____

V. Crime as Adaptive Behavior _____

VI. Modeling Theory _____

VII. Behavior Theory _____

VIII. Attachment Theory _____

IX. Self-Control Theory _____

X. Insanity and the Law _____

    A. The *M'Naughten* Rule _____

    B. The Irresistible-Impulse Test _____

    C. The *Durham* Rule _____

    D. The Substantial-Capacity Test _____

Chapter 6   Psychological and Psychiatric Foundations of Criminal Behavior

    E. The *Brawner* Rule _____

    F. Guilty but Mentally Ill _____

    G. Federal Provisions for Hospitalization of Individuals Found "NGRI" _____

 XI. Social Policy and Forensic Psychology _____

   A. Social Policy and the Psychology of Criminal Conduct _____

 XII. Criminal Psychological Profiling _____

DISCUSSION QUESTIONS

These discussion questions appear in the textbook at the end of the chapter. Your instructor may want to focus on these questions at the conclusion of the lecture on Chapter 6.

1. This book emphasizes a social problems versus social responsibility theme. Which perspective is best supported by psychological theories of crime causation? Why?

2. How do psychological theories of criminal behavior differ from the other types of theories presented in this book? How do the various psychological and psychiatric approaches presented in this chapter differ from one another?

3. How would the perspectives discussed in this chapter suggest that offenders might be prevented from committing additional offenses? How might they be rehabilitated?

4. How can crime be a form of adaptation to one's environment? Why would an individual choose such a form of adaptation over others that might be available?

5. Which of the various standards for judging legal insanity discussed in this chapter do you find the most useful? Why?

STUDENT EXERCISES

Activity 1

Your instructor will assign you a state. Go to the Web site of the Cornell University Law School's Legal Information Institute at http://www.law.cornell.edu/statutes.html, locate the statutes for this state, and find the legal definition of insanity. Answer the following questions:

1. What test or tests are used to determine legal insanity?

2. Is the defendant presumed to be sane until proven otherwise?

3. Does the burden of proof for the defense of insanity lie with the defense or the prosecution?

4. If legal insanity is proved, what verdict is used, NGRI or GBI?

Activity 2

Your instructor will place you in groups. Within your group, discuss different ways that you were taught right from wrong as a child. Using behavior theory, classify these techniques as positive rewards, negative rewards, positive punishments, or negative punishments. Which of the four types of rewards and punishments seemed to be most effective?

CRIMINOLOGY TODAY ON THE WEB

http://www.psych.org/public_info/insanity.cfm
This Web site provides information on the insanity defense from the American Psychiatric Association.

http://www.forensic-psych.com/articles/artRebirth.html
This Web site provides an article on forensic psychiatry and the insanity defense.

http://www.mentalhealth.com/dis/p20-pe04.html
http://health.discovery.com/diseasesandcond/encyclopedia/2797.html
These two sites provide information on antisocial personality disorder.

http://www.fbi.gov/majcases/jiltedmain/jiltedmain.htm
This Web site describes a FBI case involving psychological profiling.

Chapter 6 Psychological and Psychiatric Foundations of Criminal Behavior

http://faculty.ncwc.edu/toconnor/401/401lect01.htm
This Web site makes available an article on the history of profiling.

http://mentalhelp.net/mhn.htm
This site provides information on mental health, disorders, and treatments.

PRACTICE QUESTIONS

True/False

_____ 1. Poverty of affect means that the psychopath is unable to imagine accurately how others think and feel.

_____ 2. People suffering from antisocial personality disorder generally show a marked disregard for social norms and rules.

_____ 3. Psychogenic causes of antisocial personality disorder are based on physiological features of the human organism.

_____ 4. Research suggests that most convicted felons have some type of mental impairment.

_____ 5. According to Eysenck, introverts rarely become criminal offenders.

_____ 6. The Freudian concept of the ego ideal is another term for the conscience.

_____ 7. A neurosis is a serious form of mental illness.

_____ 8. Paranoid schizophrenics suffer from delusions and hallucinations.

_____ 9. When crime leads to stress reduction as a result of internal changes in beliefs and value systems, it is referred to as alloplastic adaptation.

_____ 10. According to Bandura, aggressive behavior can be learned through watching television.

_____ 11. Allowing a good child to skip homework is an example of a negative reward.

_____ 12. Persisting in the face of adversity involves performance control.

_____ 13. A defendant may be found not guilty by reason of insanity even when it is clear that the defendant committed a legally circumscribed act.

_____ 14. The end result of the *Durham* rule was to simplify the adjudication of mentally ill offenders.

_____ 15. Most crimes reported to the police are committed by only a small percentage of all offenders.

_____ 16. In their book *The Psychology of Criminal Conduct*, D. A. Andrews and James Bonta are attempting to develop a new behavioral theory.

Fill in the Blank

17. _____ is a medical subspeciality applying psychiatry to the needs of crime prevention and solution, criminal rehabilitation, and issues of criminal law.

18. The psychopath is also known as a _____.

19. Hans Eysenck's approach has been termed _____.

20. Desires, wishes, and urges emanate from the _____, according to Freud.

21. The psychological process by which one item of consciousness is symbolically substituted for another is known as _____.

22. According to J. Dollard, contact sports would be an acceptable way of expressing _____.

23. According to Gabriel Tarde, the basis of any society is _____.

24. _____ is the "stimulus–response approach" to human patterns of being.

25. The best known proponent of behavior theory is _____.

26. _____ refers to a person's ability to alter his or her own states and responses.

27. According to the Insanity Defense Reform Act, the burden of proving insanity is placed on the _____.

28. The _____ combines elements of *M'Naughten* and the irresistible-impulse test.

Multiple Choice

29. Which of the following is not a fundamental assumption of most psychological theories of crime causation?
    a. The majority motivational element within a person is personality.
    b. Defective mental processes may have a variety of causes.
    c. Crimes result from individual choice.
    d. Normality is generally defined by social consensus.

30. The concept of a psychopathic personality was developed by
    a. Hans Eysenck.
    b. Ivan Pavlov.
    c. Hervey Cleckley.
    d. Albert Bandura.

31. A possible psychogentic cause of antisocial personality disorder is
    a. a low state of arousal.
    b. a separation from the mother during the first six months of life.
    c. a malfunction of some inhibitory mechanisms.
    d. none of the above

32. Which of the following was not one of the three personality dimensions described by Hans Eysenck in his study of personality characteristics and crime?
    a. Extroversion
    b. Schizophrenism
    c. Psychoticism
    d. Neuroticism

33. According to Freud's psychoanalytic theory, the id conforms to the
    a. reality principle.
    b. pleasure principle.
    c. morality and conscience.
    d. unconscious mind.

34. The Freudian concept of a death instinct is called
    a. sublimination.
    b. ego-ideal.
    c. neurosis.
    d. Thanatos.

Chapter 6 Psychological and Psychiatric Foundations of Criminal Behavior 77

35. A(n) _____ is a form of mental illness in which a person is said to be out of touch with reality in some fundamental way.
    a. psychosis
    b. operant behavior
    c. sociopath
    d. neurosis

36. When crime leads to stress reduction as a result of internal changes in beliefs and value systems, it is known as _____ adaptation.
    a. alternative
    b. alloplastic
    c. antiplastic
    d. autoplastic

37. _____ is a psychological perspective that suggests people learn how to behave by modeling themselves after others.
    a. Social learning theory
    b. Operant behavior theory
    c. Psychoanalysis
    d. Forensic psychological theory

38. Spanking a bad child is an example of a
    a. positive reward.
    b. negative reward.
    c. positive punishment.
    d. negative punishment.

39. Attachment theory suggests that _____ attachment results in feelings of uncertainty which cause the child to feel anxious, to become fearful of its environment, and to cling to potential caregivers.
    a. anxious avoidant
    b. insecure
    c. anxious resistant
    d. secure

40. The _____ is a standard for judging legal insanity which considers whether a person was not able to resist committing the crime because of his or her mental state.
    a. *Durham* rule
    b. substantial-capacity test
    c. irresistible-impulse test
    d. *Brawner* rule

41. The jury determines what constitutes insanity in states that use the
    a. *Durham* rule.
    b. substantial-capacity test.
    c. irresistible-impulse test.
    d. *Brawner* rule.

WORD SEARCH PUZZLE

Cleckley
Conditioning
Dangerousness
Eysenck
Freud
Id
Insanity
Neurosis

Profiling
Psychopath
Psychosis
Schizophrenia
Sociopath
Sublimination
Superego

```
S C H I Z O P H R E N I A G K
U S U B L I M I N A T I O N F
P O E G C S H K H Z K A X I C
E C O N D I T I O N I N G L S
R I F E S D A U H H J V E I K
E O Q U X U P Q W G S C S F V
G P O R F E O N T B K O R O O
O A A O O R H R K L H E P R T
C T V S A F C L E C A F B P I
I H A I K U Y Y Y G N Q Y K D
N S P S T W S S W B N E H V N
P X W Q P B P Y T I N A S N I
I S F V B W G V V Z T P D Y H
T J P Z S T H O U V K E B R E
```

Chapter 6 Psychological and Psychiatric Foundations of Criminal Behavior

CROSSWORD PUZZLE

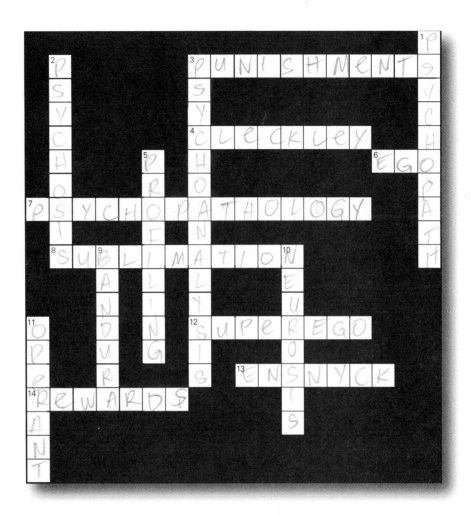

Across

3. Undesirable behavioral consequences likely to decrease the frequency of a behavior.
4. He developed the concept of a psychopathic personality.
6. The reality-testing part of the personality.
7. The study of mental illness.
8. Symbolically substituting one aspect of consciousness for another.
12. The moral aspect of the personality.
13. The author of *Crime and Personality*.
14. Desirable behavioral consequences likely to increase the frequency of a behavior.

Down

1. A person with a personality disorder manifested in aggressive antisocial behavior.
2. A mental illness in which sufferers are out of touch with reality.
3. Freud's theory of human psychology.
5. Attempts to categorize and predict the behavior of certain types of offenders.
9. He developed a comprehensive modeling theory of aggression.
10. A functional disorder of the mind.
11. _____ behavior affects the environment to produce responses.

Sociological Theories I: Social Structure

CHAPTER 7

Learning Objectives

After reading this chapter, you should be able to:

1. Explain how the organization and structure of society may contribute to criminality
2. Identify the role that cultural differences play in crime causation
3. Distinguish between a number of social-structure theories of criminal behavior
4. Identify modern-day social policy that reflects the social-structure approach
5. Assess the shortcomings of the social-structure approach

CHAPTER SUMMARY

This chapter begins with an introduction to the general assumptions of sociological theories before focusing specifically on social structure theories, theories that explain crime as the result of the institutional structure of society. The three main types of social structure theories are social disorganization theories, strain theories, and culture conflict perspectives.

Social disorganization or ecological theories are associated with the Chicago School of criminology. Robert Park and Ernest Burgess viewed cities in terms of concentric zones, with Zone II, surrounding the city center, seen as the zone of transition. Clifford Shaw and Henry McKay applied concentric zone theory to crime and found that rates of offending remained fairly constant within the zone of transition despite the arrival of various new immigrant groups. The most important contribution of the ecological school to criminology is its claim that the community has a major influence on human behavior. Recently, the emergence of environmental criminology or the criminology of place has revived ecological approaches. The broken windows thesis holds that physical deterioration in an area leads to increased concerns for personal safety among area residents and to higher crime rates in that area. The concept of defensible space is used by the criminology of place as a mechanism for reducing the risk of crime.

Strain theories see delinquency as adaptive behavior committed in response to problems involving frustrating and undesirable social environments. Classic strain theory was developed by Robert K. Merton, who developed the concept of anomie as a disjunction between socially approved means to success and legitimate goals. He outlined five modes of adaptation, or combinations of goals and means, and suggested that innovation was the mode most likely to be associated with crime. Stephen Messner and Richard Rosenfeld developed a contemporary version of Merton's theory, based on the concept of relative deprivation, the economic and social gap between rich and poor living in close proximity to one another. General strain theory, developed by Robert Agnew, reformulated strain theory and suggested that delinquency is a coping mechanism that helps adolescents deal with socio-emotional problems generated by negative social reactions.

Culture conflict or cultural deviance theory suggests that crime results from a clash of values between differently socialized groups over what is acceptable or proper behavior. Thorsten Sellin suggests that conduct norms are acquired early in life through childhood socialization. Primary conflict occurs when there is a fundamental clash of cultures, while secondary conflict occurs when smaller cultures within a primary one clash. Subcultural theory emphasizes the contribution to crime made by variously socialized cultural groups within a primary culture. Walter Miller identified focal concerns or key values of delinquent subcultures which encourage delinquent behavior. On the other hand, Gresham Sykes and David Matza suggest that offenders use techniques of neutralization to negate the norms and values of the larger society and overcome feelings of guilt at committing criminal acts. Franco Ferracuti and Marvin Wolfgang postulated the existence of violent subcultures, which are built around values that support and encourage violence. Differential opportunity theory, developed by Richard Cloward and Lloyd Ohlin, combine elements of subcultural and strain theories to suggest that delinquency may result from the availability of illegitimate opportunities for success combined with the effective replacement of the norms of the primary culture with expedient subcultural rules. Albert Cohen also combined elements of strain theory and the subcultural perspective in his theory of reaction formation, which states that juveniles who are held accountable to middle-class norms and who cannot achieve these norms may reject middle-class goals and turn to delinquency instead.

The gangs studied by early researchers were involved primarily in petty theft, vandalism, and turf battles; modern gangs are involved in more serious and violent crimes and drug dealing. However, recent researchers draw a distinction between juvenile delinquency and gang-related violence, suggesting that they are ecologically distinct community problems.

Social structure theories have influenced social policy, through programs such as the Chicago Area Project, Mobilization for Youth, and the War on Poverty. The social structural perspective is closely associated with the social problems approach and negates the claims of the social responsibility perspective. The chapter discusses a number of critiques of each type of social structure theory.

Chapter 7 Sociological Theories I: Social Structure

KEY CONCEPTS

anomie A social condition in which norms are uncertain or lacking.

broken windows thesis A perspective on crime causation which holds that physical deterioration in an area leads to increased concerns for personal safety among area residents and to higher crime rates in that area.(7)

Chicago Area Project A program focusing on urban ecology, and originating at the University of Chicago during the 1930s, which attempted to reduce delinquency, crime, and social disorganization in transitional neighborhoods.

conduct norms The shared expectations of a social group relative to personal conduct.

cultural transmission The transmission of delinquency through successive generations of people living in the same area through a process of social communication.

culture conflict theory A sociological perspective on crime which suggests that the root cause of criminality can be found in a clash of values between variously socialized groups over what is acceptable or proper behavior.

defensible space The range of mechanisms that combine to bring an environment under the control of its residents.

distributive justice The rightful, equitable, and just distribution of rewards within a society.

ecological theory A type of sociological approach which emphasizes demographics (the characteristics of population groups) and geographics (the mapped location of such groups relative to one another) and which sees the social disorganization that characterizes delinquency areas as a major cause of criminality and victimization. Also called *Chicago School of criminology*.

environmental criminology An emerging perspective which emphasizes the importance of geographic location and architectural features as they are associated with the prevalence of criminal victimization. (Note: As the term has been understood to date, environmental criminology is not the study of environmental crime, but rather a perspective that stresses how crime varies from place to place.) Also called *criminology of place*.

focal concern A key value of any culture, especially a key value of a delinquent subculture.

illegitimate opportunity structure Subcultural pathways to success which the wider society disapproves of.

opportunity structure A path to success. Opportunity structures may be of two types: legitimate and illegitimate.

reaction formation The process by which a person openly rejects that which he or she wants or aspires to but cannot obtain or achieve.

relative deprivation A sense of social or economic inequality experienced by those who are unable, for whatever reason, to achieve legitimate success within the surrounding society.

social disorganization A condition said to exist when a group is faced with social change, uneven development of culture, maladaptiveness, disharmony, conflict, and lack of consensus.

social disorganization theory A perspective on crime and deviance which sees society as a kind of organism and crime and deviance as a kind of disease or social pathology. Theories of social disorganization are often associated with the perspective of social ecology and with the Chicago School of criminology which developed during the 1920s and 1930s.

social ecology An approach to criminological theorizing that attempts to link the structure and organization of human community to interactions with its localized environment.

social life The ongoing and (typically) structured interaction that occurs between persons in a society, including socialization and social behavior in general.

social pathology A concept that compares society to a physical organism and that sees criminality as an illness.

social process The interaction between and among social institutions, individuals and groups.

social structure The pattern of social organization and the interrelationships between institutions characteristic of a society.

social structure theory A theory that explains crime by reference to some aspect of the social fabric. These theories emphasize relationships between social institutions and describe the types of behavior which tend to characterize groups of people rather than individuals.

sociological theory A perspective that focuses on the nature of the power relationships that exist between social groups and on the influences that various social phenomena bring to bear on the types of behaviors that tend to characterize groups of people.

strain theory A sociological approach which posits a disjuncture between socially and subculturally sanctioned means and goals as the cause of criminal behavior. Also called *anomie theory*.

subcultural theory A sociological perspective that emphasizes the contribution made by variously socialized cultural groups to the phenomenon of crime.

subculture A collection of values and preferences which is communicated to subcultural participants through a process of socialization.

technique of neutralization A culturally available justification which can provide criminal offenders with the means to disavow responsibility for their behavior.

CHAPTER OUTLINE

    I. Introduction _____

    II. Major Principles of Sociological Theories _____

    III. Social Structure Theories _____

    IV. Types of Social Structure Theories _____

        A. Social Disorganization Theory _____

Chapter 7 Sociological Theories I: Social Structure

        B. Strain Theory _____

        _____

        C. Culture Conflict Theory _____

        _____

   V. Policy Implications of Social Structure Theories _____

      _____

  VI. Critique of Social Structure Theories _____

      _____

DISCUSSION QUESTIONS

These discussion questions are found in the textbook at the end of the chapter. Your instructor may want to focus on these questions at the conclusion of the lecture on Chapter 7.

1. What is the nature of sociological theorizing? What are the assumptions upon which sociological perspectives on crime causation rest?

2. What are the three key sociological explanations for crime that are discussed at the beginning of this chapter? How do they differ from one another?

3. What are the three types of social structure theories that this chapter describes? What are the major differences between them?

4. Do you believe that ecological approaches have a valid place in contemporary criminological thinking? Why or why not?

5. How, if at all, does the notion of a criminology of place differ from more traditional ecological theories? Do you see the criminology of place approach as capable of offering anything new over traditional approaches? If so, what?

6. What is a violent subculture? Why do some subcultures stress violence? How might participants in a subculture of violence be turned toward less aggressive ways?

7. This book emphasizes a social problems versus social responsibility theme. Which of the theoretical perspectives discussed in this chapter best support the social problems approach? Which support the social responsibility approach? Why?

8. What are the policy implications of the theories discussed in this chapter? What kinds of changes in society and in government policy might be based on the theories discussed here? Would they be likely to bring about a reduction in crime?

STUDENT EXERCISES

Activity 1

Obtain official crime data from the UCR on crime in various neighborhoods in a large city near you. Plot the crime data on a county map. Do you see a pattern? Discuss whether concentric zone theory fits the crime distribution in your city.

Activity 2

Your instructor will divide the class into groups. Discuss the subcultures to which members of the group belong. What norms and values of each subculture might conflict with the norms and values of the larger culture? Might any of these clashes lead to crime, delinquency, or deviance? How?

CRIMINOLOGY TODAY ON THE WEB

http://www.gothics.org/subculture
This Web site provides a detailed description of the gothic subculture, a modern subculture present in American society.

http://faculty.washington.edu/bridges/soc271/lectures/presentation3/sld001.htm
This Web site provides a slide presentation of how social structure is linked to deviant behavior. It mentions many of the theories discussed in this chapter of the text.

http://social-sciences.uchicago.edu/ssdnews/fixing.html
This Web site provides an article on a recent study examining the broken windows thesis.

http://www.journals.uchicago.edu/AJS/home.html
This Web site provides online access to the *American Journal of Sociology*, which includes research on theories discussed in this and other chapters in the text.

http://www.ncjrs.org/html/ojjdp/97_ygs/contents.html
This Web site provides the results of the 1997 National Youth Gang Survey.

http://www.iir.com/nygc
This is the home page of the National Youth Gang Center.

http://www.albany.edu/scj/jcjpc
This is the home page of the *Journal of Criminal Justice and Popular Culture*. Volume 3 contains material on culture, crime, and cultural criminology.

Chapter 7 Sociological Theories I: Social Structure

PRACTICE QUESTIONS

True/False

_____ 1. Sociological approaches generally use a micro perspective.

_____ 2. Strain theories are also known as ecological approaches.

_____ 3. According to Shaw and McKay, rates of offending within zones of transition changed over time.

_____ 4. Environmental criminology emphasizes the relationship between location and the prevalence of victimization.

_____ 5. Places cannot be criminogenic in and of themselves.

_____ 6. One's perception of the rightful distribution of rewards depends on cultural expectations.

_____ 7. One of the factors that determines whether a person will respond to strain in a criminal or conforming manner is intelligence.

_____ 8. According to Thorsten Sellin, conduct norms are acquired early in life.

_____ 9. According to Miller, subcultural crime and deviance are direct consequences of poverty and lack of opportunity.

_____ 10. Claiming that the authorities are corrupt is an example of the technique of neutralization known as condemning the condemners.

_____ 11. Techniques of neutralization allow delinquents to participate in crime without being fully alienated from the larger society.

_____ 12. Participants in a violent subculture use techniques of neutralization to deal with feelings of guilty about their aggression.

_____ 13. According to differential opportunity theory, a lower-class youth who becomes addicted to drugs is probably involved in a conflict subculture.

_____ 14. Gang crime during the 1920s involved primarily vandalism and petty theft.

_____ 15. Most gangs are racially exclusive.

_____ 16. Social structural theories are consistent with the social problems approach.

Fill in the Blank

17. Seeing crime as the product of class struggle is characteristic of _____ theories.

18. According to Park and Burgess, Zone _____ was the commuter zone.

19. _____ data are gathered in the form of life stories.

20. According to Merton, _____ is a disjunction between socially approved means to success and legitimate goals.

21. The social gap between rich and poor living in close proximity to one another is known as _____.

22. Culture conflict theory is also known as _____ theory.

23. A subculture is communicated to participants through a process of _____.

24. According to Ferracuti and Wolfgang, the _____ involves legitimizing the use of violence as an appropriate way to resolve social conflicts.

25. People who openly reject what they want but cannot obtain are engaging in _____.

26. Social structure theories negate the claims of the social _____ perspective.

Multiple Choice

27. Social _____ theories examine institutional arrangements within society.
    a. structure
    b. life
    c. process
    d. pathology

28. Social disorganization theory is closely associated with the _____ school of criminology.
    a. classical
    b. positivist
    c. ecological
    d. conflict

29. The concentric zone model was applied to the study of delinquency by
    a. Clifford Shaw and Henry McKay.
    b. Robert Park and Ernest Burgess.
    c. W.I. Thomas and Florian Znaniecki.
    d. Steven Messner and Richard Rosenfeld.

30. Early ecological theories of crime were collectively referred to as the _____ School of Criminology.
    a. Classical
    b. Positivist
    c. Chicago
    d. New York

31. Merton's strain theory stresses
    a. the idea that although criminal behavior is not inherited, tendencies toward criminal behavior are inherited.
    b. the importance of a person's early family environment in determining attitudes toward crime.
    c. the sexual maladjustments of people as a main source of crime.
    d. the idea that American society emphasizes common success goals without providing equal access to the means of obtaining them.

32. _____ is a person's perception of his or her rightful place in the reward structure of society.
    a. Relative deprivation
    b. Distributive justice
    c. Focal concerns
    d. Cultural transmission

33. According to general strain theory, strain occurs when which of the following events occurs?
    a. Someone tries to prevent you from achieving positively valued goals.
    b. Someone removes negatively valued stimuli.
    c. Someone presents you with positively valued stimuli.
    d. Someone helps you to achieve positively valued goals.

Chapter 7 Sociological Theories I: Social Structure

34. _____ theory is a sociological perspective that emphasizes the contribution made by variously socialized cultural groups to the phenomenon of crime.
    a. Conflict
    b. Strain
    c. Subcultural
    d. Anomie

35. Which of the following is not one of Miller's focal concerns?
    a. Trouble
    b. Toughness
    c. Autonomy
    d. Control

36. The technique of neutralization which involves a young offender claiming that the unlawful acts were "not my fault" is known as
    a. denial of injury.
    b. denial of responsibility.
    c. appeal to higher loyalties.
    d. condemnation of the condemners.

37. It appears that certain forms of violence are more acceptable in the _____ portion of the United States.
    a. northeastern
    b. southern
    c. western
    d. midwestern

38. According to Cloward and Ohlin, a Type _____ youth wants to desire wealth but not entry into the middle class.
    a. I
    b. II
    c. III
    d. IV

39. Reaction formation was developed by
    a. Albert Cohen.
    b. Thorsten Sellin.
    c. David Matza.
    d. Robert Agnew.

40. Some researchers suggest that _____ theories fail to distinguish between the condition of social disorganization and the crimes that this condition is said to cause.
    a. ecological
    b. strain
    c. culture conflict
    d. subcultural

WORD SEARCH PUZZLE

Anomie
Burgess
Chicago
Ecological
Ferracuti
McKay
Opportunity

Park
Sellin
Shaw
Sociological
Subculture
Wolfgang

```
S O D E J S P Y H W Y P I A
O Q X C S U F A F K G A D Y
C P P O O B E D G W V R A K
I Y P L T C R W O Q X K P A
O E S O O U R M M V C O D Z
L O Z G R L A N O M I E Q V
O G W I F T C B D Y B J I D
G A N C C U U Q V H K E G H
I C I A W R T N M N Y F H U
C I I L G E I Y I Q W S Q Y
A H P E X F J L F T M U O V
L C S Y R B L Q N U Y L M P
U S W E U E B O T Y D H M B
B W A H S K D X W E N T V N
```

Chapter 7 Sociological Theories I: Social Structure

CROSSWORD PUZZLE

Across

3. Relative _____ refers to the gap between rich and poor living in close proximity.
5. A collection of values communicated to participants through a process of socialization.
6. Miller's theory of _____ concerns focused on delinquent subcultures.
8. Social disorganization theory is associated with the _____ school of criminology.
10. A theory developed by Robert Merton.
12. A disjunction between means and goals.
13. General strain theory was developed by Robert _____.
14. Ferracuti and _____ developed the concept of violent subcultures.
15. They type of conflict occurring when smaller cultures within the primary one clash.

Down

1. Sykes and Matza proposed five techniques of _____.
2. The most common mode of adaptation.
4. Park and _____ viewed cities in terms of concentric zones.
7. Cohen proposed the concept of _____ formation.
9. The mode of adaptation most associated with crime.
11. According to Sellin, conduct _____ provide the valuative basis for human behavior

sociological theories II: social process and social development

Learning Objectives

After reading this chapter, you should be able to:

1. Recognize how the process of social interaction between people contributes to criminal behavior
2. Identify and distinguish between a number of social process and social development perspectives
3. Identify current social policy initiatives that reflect the social development approach
4. Assess the shortcomings of the social process and social development perspectives

CHAPTER SUMMARY

This chapter begins with an introduction to social process theories or interactionist perspectives, which assume that everyone has the potential to violate the law, so that criminality is not an innate characteristic of certain individuals. The main types of social process theories are social learning theory, social control theory, labeling theory, the reintegrative shaming approach, and dramaturgy.

Learning theories suggest that crime, like all other types of behavior, is learned. One of the most influential learning theories is differential association, which was developed by Edwin Sutherland and which suggests that criminality is learned through a process of differential association with others who communicate criminal values and advocate the commission of crimes. Differential association-reinforcement theory adds the idea of reinforcement to Sutherland's theory; Robert Burgess and Ronald L. Akers integrated the concept of operant conditioning. Another theory building on Sutherland's work is Daniel Glaser's differential identification theory, which suggests that the process of differential association leads to an intimate personal identification with offenders, resulting in criminal acts.

Social control theories ask why people obey the laws instead of committing crimes. Containment theory, developed by Walter Reckless, suggests that individuals have control mechanisms, or containments, which protect them from crime; if these containments fail, people become vulnerable to criminal behavior. Howard Kaplan proposed the self-derogation theory of delinquency, which suggests that low self-esteem may promote delinquency, and that delinquent behavior may enhance self-esteem. Social bond theory, as proposed by Travis Hirschi, suggests that when the bond between an individual and a social group is weakened or broken, deviance and crime may result. Hirschi and Michael Gottfredson later proposed a general theory of crime which emphasized the lack of self-control as the key factor in explaining all types of crime. Charles Tittle's control-balance theory blends social bond and containment theory and includes the concept of a control ratio, which purports to predict not only the probability that one will engage in deviance but also the form that deviance will take.

Labeling theory focuses on society's reaction to deviance. Frank Tannenbaum developed the term *tagging* to explain how offenders become identified as bad and unredeemable after undergoing processing through the criminal justice system. The concepts of primary deviance (the offender's initial acts of deviance) and secondary deviance (continued acts of deviance) as developed by Edwin M. Lemert describe the development of a criminal career as a result of being tagged with the status of criminal. Howard Becker expanded on the labeling perspective, emphasizing that no act is intrinsically deviant, but must be so defined by society.

The concept of reintegrative shaming, developed by John Braithwaite, describes processes by which a deviant is labeled and sanctioned by society, but is then brought back into a community of conformity. According to Braithwaite, whereas stigmatic shaming destroys the moral bond between the offender and the community, reintegrative shaming strengthens the bond.

Finally, the dramaturgical perspective, developed by Erving Goffman, suggests that individuals play a variety of nearly simultaneous social roles which must be sustained in interaction with others. If discrediting information, or information that a person wants to hide, is revealed, the flow of interaction is disrupted and the nature of the performance may be changed substantially.

Social policy theories have influenced social policy through programs such as the Juvenile Mentoring Program, Preparing for the Drug Free Years, and the Montreal Preventive Treatment Program. The chapter discusses a number of critiques of each type of social policy theory.

Because the social development perspective focuses on human development on many levels, social development theories tend to be integrated theories. Major concepts in social development theories are discussed.

The life course perspective, developed by Robert J. Sampson and John Laub, focuses on the development of criminal careers over the life course and how these careers both start and

Chapter 8 Sociological Theories II: Social Process and Social Development

finish. Laub and Sampson's age-graded theory involved reanalysis of data collected by Sheldon and Eleanor Glueck and emphasizes two key events in the life course (marriage and job stability) that seem to be particularly important in reducing the frequency of offending in later life.

Terrie Moffitt's dual taxonomic theory attempts to explain why, although adult criminality is almost always preceded by antisocial behavior during adolescence, most antisocial children do not become adult offenders. The theory discusses how positive developmental pathways may be fostered in adolescence. David P. Farrington and Donald J. West studied the issue of when offenders desist from crime. Other researchers using cohort analysis to study criminal careers include Marvin Wolfgang, who found that a small number of violent offenders were responsible for most of the crimes committed by the cohort. Lawrence E. Cohen and Richard Machalek developed the evolutionary ecology perspective, which attempts to explain how people acquire criminality, when and why they express it as crime, how individuals and groups respond to those crimes, and how this all interacts as a system evolving over time.

A number of researchers are focusing on developmental pathways leading to criminality. The Program of Research on the Causes and Correlates of Delinquency is conducting a number of longitudinal studies of youth throughout their developmental years to understand the causes of delinquency and how it may be prevented. The Project on Human Development in Chicago Neighborhoods is a longitudinal study of how individuals, families, institutions, and communities evolve together and is tracing how criminal behavior evolves from birth to age 32.

Social development theories have influenced social policy. It is the foundation for the OJJDP's Comprehensive Strategy Program and for the Boys and Girls Clubs of America's Targeted Outreach program. The chapter discusses a number of critiques of social development theories.

KEY CONCEPTS

Cambridge Study in Delinquent Development A longitudinal (life course) study of crime and delinquency tracking a cohort of 411 boys born in London in 1953.

cohort analysis A social scientific technique which studies over time a population that shares common characteristics. Cohort analysis usually begins at birth and traces the development of cohort members until they reach a certain age.

containment Aspects of the social bond which act to prevent individuals from committing crimes and which keep them from engaging in deviance.

containment theory A form of control theory which suggests that a series of both internal and external factors contributes to law-abiding behavior.

control ratio The amount of control to which a person is subject versus the amount of control that person exerts over others.

criminal career The longitudinal sequence of crimes committed by an individual offender.

desistance The cessation of criminal activity or the termination of a period of involvement in offending behavior.

differential association The sociological thesis that criminality, like any other form of behavior, is learned through a process of association with others who communicate criminal values.

differential identification theory An explanation for crime and deviance which holds that people pursue criminal or deviant behavior to the extent that they identify themselves with real or imaginary people from whose perspective their criminal or deviant behavior seems acceptable.

discrediting information Information that is inconsistent with the managed impressions being communicated in a given situation.

dramaturgical perspective A theoretical point of view that depicts human behavior as centered around the purposeful management of interpersonal impressions. Also called *dramaturgy*.

evolutionary ecology An approach to understanding crime that draws attention to the ways people develop over the course of their lives.

human development The relationship between the maturing individual and his or her changing environment, as well as the social processes that the relationship entails.

impression management The intentional enactment of practiced behavior which is intended to convey to others one's desirable personal characteristics and social qualities.

labeling An interactionist perspective which sees continued crime as a consequence of limited opportunities for acceptable behavior which follow from the negative responses of society to those defined as offenders. Also, the process by which a negative or deviant label is imposed.

learning theory (sociology) A perspective that places primary emphasis upon the role of communication and socialization in the acquisition of learned patterns of criminal behavior and the values that support that behavior.

life course Pathways through the age-differentiated life span. Also, the course of a person's life over time.

moral enterprise The efforts made by an interest group to have its sense of moral or ethical propriety enacted into law.

Office of Juvenile Justice and Delinquency Prevention (OJJDP) A national office that provides monetary assistance and direct victim service programs for juvenile courts.

persistence Continuity in crime. Also, continual involvement in offending.

primary deviance Initial deviance often undertaken to deal with transient problems in living.

Project on Human Development in Chicago Neighborhoods (PHDCN) An intensive study of Chicago neighborhoods employing longitudinal evaluations to examine the changing circumstances of people's lives in an effort to identify personal characteristics that may lead toward or away from antisocial behavior.

reintegrative shaming A form of shaming, imposed as a sanction by the criminal justice system, that is thought to strengthen the moral bond between the offender and the community.

secondary deviance Deviant behavior which results from official labeling and from association with others who have been so labeled.

social bond The link, created through socialization, between individuals and the society of which they are a part.

Chapter 8 Sociological Theories II: Social Process and Social Development

social capital The degree of positive relationships with others and with social institutions that individuals build up over the course of their lives.

social control theory A perspective which predicts that when social constraints on antisocial behavior are weakened or absent, delinquent behavior emerges. Rather than stressing causative factors in criminal behavior, control theory asks why people actually obey rules instead of breaking them.

social development perspective An integrated view of human development that examines multiple levels of maturation simultaneously, including the psychological, biological, familial, interpersonal, cultural, societal, and ecological levels.

social learning theory A psychological perspective that says that people learn how to behave by modeling themselves after others whom they have the opportunity to observe.

social process theory A theory that asserts that criminal behavior is learned in interaction with others and that socialization processes that occur as the result of group membership are the primary route through which learning occurs. Also called *interactionist perspective*.

stigmatic shaming A form of shaming, imposed as a sanction by the criminal justice system, that is thought to destroy the moral bond between the offender and the community.

tagging The process whereby an individual is negatively defined by agencies of justice. Also called *labeling*.

CHAPTER OUTLINE

I. Introduction _____

II. The Social Process Perspective _____

III. Types of Social Process Approaches _____

    A. Learning Theory _____

    B. Social Control Theory _____

    C. Labeling Theory _____

    D. Reintegrative Shaming _____

    E. Dramaturgy _____

IV. Policy Implications of Social Process Theories _____

V. Critique of Social Process Theories _____
_____

VI. The Social Development Perspective _____
_____

VII. Concepts in Social Development Theories _____
_____

   A. The Life Course Perspective _____
   _____

   B. Laub and Sampson's Age-Graded Theory _____
   _____

   C. Moffitt's Dual Taxonomic Theory _____
   _____

   D. Farrington's Delinquent Development Theory _____
   _____

   E. Evolutionary Ecology _____
   _____

   F. Developmental Pathways _____
   _____

   G. The Chicago Human Development Project _____
   _____

VIII. Policy Implications of Social Development Theories _____
_____

IX. Critique of Social Development Theories _____
_____

DISCUSSION QUESTIONS

These discussion questions are found in the textbook at the end of the chapter. Your instructor may want to focus on these questions at the conclusion of the lecture on Chapter 8

1. This chapter describes both social process and social development perspectives. What are the significant differences between these two perspectives? What kinds of theories characterize each?

2. This textbook emphasizes a social problems versus social responsibility theme. Which of the perspectives discussed in this chapter (if any) best support the social problems approach? Which (if any) support the social responsibility approach? Why?

3. This chapter contains a discussion of the labeling process. Give a few examples of the everyday imposition of positive, rather than negative, labels. Why is it so difficult to impose positive labels on individuals who were previously labeled negatively?

4. Do you believe that Erving Goffman's dramaturgical approach, which sees the world as a stage and individuals as actors upon that stage, provides any valuable insights into crime and criminality? If so, what are they?

5. What kinds of social policy initiatives might be suggested by social process theories? By social development theories? Which do you think might be most effective? Why?

6. What are the shortcomings of the social process perspective? Of the social development perspective?

STUDENT EXERCISES

Activity 1

Your instructor will divide the class into groups and assign your group one of the theories discussed in this chapter. Develop a crime reduction and/or prevention policy that is based on this theory. Explain how the theory justifies the policy and why you expect the policy to reduce or prevent crime.

Activity 2

According to Hirschi's social bond theory, four elements of a social bond work together to promote law-abiding behavior and prevent involvement in crime and delinquency: attachment, commitment, involvement, and belief. Explain how youth organizations such as the Boy Scouts, Girl Scouts, and 4-H Clubs (or similar groups) work to strengthen these four elements of the social bond and encourage members to engage in normative behaviors.

Activity 3

Currently, there is considerable debate over the belief that violent video games may lead to criminal behavior among juveniles. Explain how this belief could be supported by the theories discussed in this chapter.

CRIMINOLOGY TODAY ON THE WEB

http://www.sonoma.edu/cja/info/Edintro.html

This Web site was created in memory of Edwin Lemert, who died in 1996. It includes links to some of his articles and to an interview with him.

http://www.aber.ac.uk/media/Functions/mcs.html

This Web site, which is part of the University of Wales, Aberystwyth Media and Communications Program, includes links to articles and other information on the relationship between television and violence.

http://www.preventingcrime.org/report

This site makes available a comprehensive report on the effectiveness of crime prevention that was mandated by Congress in 1996. It includes information on the relationship between various theories of crime causation and public policy, including many of the theories discussed in this chapter.

http://personal.tmlp.com/ddemelo/crime/differ.html

This Web site provides a discussion of Sutherland's theory of differential association.

http://www.geocities.com/CollegePark/Quad/5889

The article at this site discusses Erving Goffman's dramaturgy perspective.

http://www.crimetheory.com/Archive/Response/index.html

This site includes a discussion of various "social response" theories, including labeling theory.

PRACTICE QUESTIONS

True/False

_____ 1. Sutherland suggested that criminality occurs when there is a disjunction of socially approved goals and legitimate means.

_____ 2. According to Akers, differential reinforcement is also known as imitation.

_____ 3. According to Glaser, a role model must be an actual person.

_____ 4. Containment theory was developed by Howard Becker.

_____ 5. A perceived reward that may be offered by crime is an external containment.

_____ 6. Hirschi and Gottfredson's theory is based on a rational choice perspective.

_____ 7. Deviance engendered by a control deficit usually takes the form of decadence and exploitation.

_____ 8. Secondary deviance is usually undertaken to solve an immediate problem or to meet the expectations of one's subcultural group.

Chapter 8 Sociological Theories II: Social Process and Social Development 101

_____ 9. Essentially, labeling theory denies the concept of *male in se*.

_____ 10. A secret deviant is not guilty but has still been labeled deviant.

_____ 11. According to Goffman, dramatic realization occurs when impression management has been successful.

_____ 12. According to theories of social development, a critical transitional period occurs as a person moves from childhood to adulthood.

_____ 13. The research conducted by Sheldon and Eleanor Glueck concluded that delinquent careers rarely carried over into adulthood.

_____ 14. Unaided desistance is also known as rehabilitation.

_____ 15. Independence is the final developmental task necessary for successful prosocial development during childhood and adolescence.

_____ 16. Social development theories have been criticized for definitional issues.

Fill in the Blank

17. Burgess and Akers added the concept of _____ to Sutherland's original idea of differential association.

18. Glaser suggests that identification with _____ offers the possibility of rehabilitation.

19. According to Reckless, _____ containments are more important in preventing law violations.

20. According to Hirschi, a _____ has little or no attachment to society.

21. A _____ deviant violates social norms but does not encounter any negative societal reactions.

22. A _____ is a facility from which people can come and go and in which communal life is circumscribed.

23. The _____ dimension of a criminal career refers to the fraction of the population that is criminally active.

24. Laub and Sampson's concept of _____ refers to the degree of positive relationships with other persons and with social institutions that people build up over the course of their lives.

25. The _____ perspective on crime control was pioneered by Lawrence Cohen and Richard Machalek.

26. According to Tittle, people with a control _____ can exercise a lot of control over others.

Multiple Choice

27. Social _____ theories assume that everyone has the potential to violate the law.
    a. development
    b. process
    c. structure
    d. disorganization

28. According to differential association theory, criminal behavior is
    a. inherited.
    b. learned.
    c. a function of culture conflict.
    d. none of the above

29. Differential identification theory was developed by
    a. Ronald Akers.
    b. Edwin Sutherland.
    c. Daniel Glaser.
    d. Howard B. Kaplan.

30. According to containment theory, a positive self-image is an important _____ containment.
    a. outer
    b. inner
    c. external
    d. personal

31. Social bond theory postulates that
    a. crime occurs when there is a disparity between societal goals and the legitimate means available to reach those goals.
    b. criminal behavior is learned in the same way any other type of behavior is learned.
    c. crime occurs when a person's links to society are weakened or broken, thus reducing the likelihood of conformity.
    d. crime occurs because the criminal justice system stigmatizes individuals, forcing them into a deviant lifestyle.

32. According to Hirschi and Gottfredson's general theory of crime, the key concept in explaining all forms of criminal behavior is
    a. social bonds.
    b. self-control.
    c. sensitivity.
    d. intelligence.

33. The Women's Christian Temperance Union is an early example of
    a. tagging.
    b. labeling.
    c. moral enterprise.
    d. reintegrative shaming.

34. According to Becker's typology, a person who is punished for a crime he or she did not commit is a(n) _____ deviant.
    a. pure
    b. secret
    c. falsely accused
    d. innocent

35. The dramaturgical perspective was developed by
    a. Howard Becker.
    b. Edwin Lemert.
    c. Erving Goffman.
    d. Ronald Akers.

36. Life course criminology was given its name in a seminal book written by
    a. Michael Gottfredson and Travis Hirschi.
    b. Sheldon and Eleanor Glueck.
    c. Robert Sampson and John Laub.
    d. Terrie E. Moffitt.

37. The concept of turning points in a criminal career was first identified by
    a. Sheldon and Eleanor Glueck.
    b. G.B. Trasler.
    c. Terrie E. Moffitt.
    d. Richard Machalek.

38. According to Moffit's theory, which of the following is not a positive outcome of the developmental process?
    a. Competency
    b. Connectedness
    c. Control
    d. Cohort

39. According to the Causes and Correlates study, the _____ pathway to delinquency begins with behaviors such as frequent lying or shoplifting around age 10.
    a. overt
    b. authority conflict
    c. multiple disruption
    d. covert

40. The primary goal of the _____ program is to provide a positive alternative to gangs for at-risk youth.
    a. Comprehensive Strategy
    b. PDHDCN
    c. JUMP
    d. Targeted Outreach

WORD SEARCH PUZZLE

- Cohort
- Containment
- Desistance
- Deviance
- Dramaturgy
- Farrington
- Gottfredson
- Hirschi
- labeling
- Laub
- Reckless
- Sampson
- Shaming
- Sutherland
- West
- Wolfgang

```
C A R U N D Y S A F N R S G H
G O T T F R E D S O N A N I A
N H N R Z D C V T X M I R O U
I U W T S E W G I P M S E A M
L Q O E A S N M S A C A C D Y
E E L G G I W O H H N S K O J
B X F B R S N S I U W C L H H
A Y G R U T A M A R D D E A A
L E A D N A L R E H T U S Q B
D F N H N N L P I N I R S J W
R R G G P C O H O R T T H Q R
U W I X V E P D D U G D A U L
```

Chapter 8 Sociological Theories II: Social Process and Social Development

CROSSWORD PUZZLE

Across

1. A group of people having certain significant social characteristics in common.
3. The component of a social bond that refers to a shared value and moral system.
6. _____ theory suggests that internal and external factors contribute to law-abiding behavior.
7. The creator of differential association theory.
9. The cessation of criminal activity.
10. He popularized social bond theory.
11. He developed the dramaturgical perspective.

Down

2. _____ shaming strengthens the moral bond between the offender and the community.
4. The process by which one is negatively defined by agencies of justice
5. Continuity in crime, or continual involvement in offending.
8. _____ shaming destroys the moral bond between the offender and the community.
9. A theory that sees behavior as centered around the management of interpersonal impressions.

sociological theories III: social conflict

CHAPTER 9

Learning Objectives

After reading this chapter, you should be able to:

1. Recognize the ways in which power conflict between social groups contributes to crime and criminal activity
2. Understand the distinctions between a number of social conflict theories
3. Identify those social policy initiatives that reflect the social conflict approach
4. Assess the shortcomings of the social conflict perspective

CHAPTER SUMMARY

This chapter begins with a discussion of three analytical perspectives: consensus, pluralist, and conflict. The consensus perspective is based on the premise that most members of society agree on what is right and wrong and share a set of core values. This perspective assumes that the criminal law reflects the collective will of the people and serves everyone equally, and believes that criminals are unique. The pluralist perspective assumes that there are a variety of viewpoints, values, and beliefs, but that most people agree on the usefulness of law as a formal means of dispute resolution, so that the law is a peacekeeping tool used to resolve conflict. The conflict perspective holds that there is no consensus on what is right and wrong, that conflict is a fundamental aspect of social life, and that the law is a tool of the powerful that is used to maintain their power.

Radical criminology is based on the writings of Karl Marx, who believed that conflict was inevitable in any capitalist society. George Vold helped to create this field of criminology, describing crime as the result of political conflict between groups. Other early conflict theorists included Ralf Dahrendorf and Austin Turk. Modern radical theory suggests that crime causes are rooted in social conditions empowering the wealthy and politically well organized and disenfranchising those less fortunate. William Chambliss, a modern radical criminologist, emphasizes the power gap between the powerful and powerless as helping to create crime. Richard Quinney stated that crime is inevitable under capitalist conditions. Modern radical–critical criminologists focus on promoting a gradual transition to socialized forms of government activity. Critiques of radical–critical criminology include its overemphasis on methods at the expense of well-developed theory, its failure to recognize the existence of a fair degree of public consensus about the nature of crime, and its inability to explain low crime rates in some capitalist countries or the problems existing in communist countries.

There are a variety of new innovative conflict theories. Left-realist criminology portrays crime in terms understandable to those most affected by it, shifting the focus to a pragmatic assessment of crime and the needs of victims. Key scholars include Walter DeKeseredy and Jock Young. A key principle of left realism is that radical ideas must be translated into realistic social policies. Critiques of left-realist criminology include the claim that it represents more of an ideological emphasis than a theory and the belief that realist criminologists build upon existing theoretical frameworks but rarely offer new testable propositions or hypotheses. Feminist criminology attempts to include gender awareness in the thinking of mainstream criminologists, pointing out inequities inherent in patriarchal forms of thought. Early researchers include Freda Adler and Rita J. Simon, who suggested that gender differences in crime rates were due to socialization, not biology. However, despite increased gender equality, the criminal behavior of men and women has not become more similar. Key contemporary theorists include Kathleen Daly and Meda Chesney-Lind, who are concerned about androcentricity in criminology. There are several schools of feminist thought, including radical feminism, liberal feminism, and social feminism, as well as a perspective developed by women of color emphasizing feminism's sensitivity to the interplay of gender, class, and race oppression. John Hagan developed power-control theory, which suggests that the social distribution of criminality is passed on by the family. Modern feminist thinkers suggest social policies such as increasing controls over male violence towards women, creating alternatives for women facing abuse, and the protection of children. Critiques of feminist theory suggest that it may be a theory in formation rather than a completely developed theory of crime. Some critics argue that a feminist criminology is impossible, although feminist thought may inform criminology.

Postmodern criminology applies understandings of social change inherent in postmodern philosophy to criminological theorizing and to issues of crime control. Much is deconstructionist, challenging existing criminological perspectives and working toward replacing them with perspectives more relevant to the postmodern era. Two key postmodern criminologists are Stuart Henry and Dragan Milovanovic, who focus on constitutive criminology, claiming that crime and crime control are constructions produced through a social process involving the offender, victim, and society and stating that crime should be understood as an integral part of society. Critics of postmodern theory claim that the terminology is vaguely defined and the approaches are often incoherent and confusing and that postmodernism challenges traditional theories but fails to offer feasible alternatives for crime prevention and control. Peacemaking criminology is a new form of postmodernism which suggests that citizens and social control agencies need to work together to alleviate social problems and reduce crime. Key theorists include Harold Pepinsky and Richard Quinney, who suggest that the problem of crime control is not "how to stop crime" but "how to make peace." Peacemaking emphasizes a peace model of crime control, focusing on ways of developing a shared consensus on critical issues such as crime. Programs such as dispute resolution are based on the participatory justice principle. Restorative justice is a social movement stressing healing over retribution. Peacemaking criminology has been criticized as being naive and utopian and for failing to recognize the realities of crime control and law enforcement.

Social conflict theory suggests that reducing conflict will lead to a reduction in crime rates. The various schools of thought have different views of how to reduce conflict, ranging from the use of conflict resolution to the replacement of the existing capitalist system with a socialist economic structure.

KEY CONCEPTS

androcentricity A single-sex perspective; as in the case of criminologists who study only the criminality of males.

bourgeoisie In Marxist theory, the class of people who own the means of production.

conflict perspective An analytical perspective on social organization which holds that conflict is a fundamental aspect of social life itself and can never be fully resolved.

consensus model An analytical perspective on social organization which holds that most members of society agree about what is right and what is wrong and that the various elements of society work together in unison toward a common and shared vision of the greater good.

constitutive criminology The study of the process by which human beings create an ideology of crime that sustains the notion of crime as a concrete reality.

deconstructionist theory A postmodern perspective that challenges existing criminological theories in order to debunk them and that works toward replacing traditional ideas with concepts seen as more appropriate to the postmodern era.

feminist criminology A self-conscious corrective model intended to redirect the thinking of mainstream criminologists to include gender awareness.

gender gap The observed differences between male and female rates of criminal offending in a given society, such as the United States.

instrumental Marxism A perspective which holds that those in power intentionally create laws and social institutions that serve their own interests and that keep others from becoming powerful.

justice model A contemporary model of imprisonment in which the principle of just deserts forms the underlying social philosophy.

left realism A conflict perspective that insists on a pragmatic assessment of crime and its associated problems. Also called *realist criminology*.

liberal feminism A perspective which holds that the concerns of women can be incorporated within existing social institutions through conventional means and without the need to drastically restructure society. Criminal laws, such as the Violence against Women Act, for example, have been enacted in order to change the legal structure in such a way that it becomes responsive to women's issues.

participatory justice A relatively informal type of criminal justice case processing which makes use of local community resources rather than requiring traditional forms of official intervention.

patriarchy The tradition of male dominance.

peacemaking criminology A perspective which holds that crime control agencies and the citizens they serve should work together to alleviate social problems and human suffering and thus reduce crime.

peace model An approach to crime control which focuses on effective ways for developing a shared consensus on critical issues which could seriously affect the quality of life.

pluralist perspective An analytical approach to social organization which holds that a multiplicity of values and beliefs exists in any complex society but that most social actors agree on the usefulness of law as a formal means of dispute resolution.

postmodern criminology A brand of criminology that developed following World War II and that builds on the tenets inherent in postmodern social thought.

power-control theory A perspective which holds that the distribution of crime and delinquency within society is to some degree founded upon the consequences which power relationships within the wider society hold for domestic settings and for the everyday relationships between men, women, and children within the context of family life.

proletariat In Marxist theory, the working class.

radical criminology A perspective which holds that the causes of crime are rooted in social conditions which empower the wealthy and the politically well organized but disenfranchise the less fortunate. Also called *critical criminology; Marxist criminology*.

radical feminism A perspective which holds that any significant change in the social status of women can be accomplished only through substantial changes in social institutions such as the family, law, medicine, and so on. Radical feminism argues, for example, that the structure of current legal thinking involves what is fundamentally a male perspective, which should be changed to incorporate women's social experiences and points of view.

restorative justice A postmodern perspective which stresses "remedies and restoration rather than prison, punishment and victim neglect."[1]

social class Distinctions made between individuals on the basis of important defining social characteristics.

socialist feminism A perspective which examines social roles and the gender-based division of labor within the family, seeing both as a significant source of women's subordination within society. This perspective calls for a redefinition of gender-related job status, compensation for women who work within the home, and equal pay for equal work regardless of gender.

---

1 Fay Honey Knopp, "Community Solutions to Sexual Violence: Feminist-Abolitionist Perspectives," in Harold Pepinsky and Richard Quinney, eds., *Criminology as Peacemaking* (Bloomington: Indiana University Press, 1991), p. 183.

Chapter 9 Sociological Theories III: Social Conflict

structural Marxism A perspective which holds that the structural institutions of society influence the behavior of individuals and groups by virtue of the type of relationships created. The criminal law, for example, reflects class relationships and serves to reinforce those relationships.

CHAPTER OUTLINE

I. Introduction _____

II. Law and Social Order Perspectives _____

    A. The Consensus Perspective _____

    B. The Pluralistic Perspective _____

    C. The Conflict Perspective _____

III. Radical-Critical Criminology _____

    A. Early Radical Criminology _____

    B. Radical Criminology Today _____

    C. Critical Criminology _____

    D. Radical-Critical Criminology and Policy Issues _____

    E. Critiques of Radical-Critical Criminology _____

IV. Emerging Conflict Theories _____

    A. Left-Realist Criminology _____

    B. Feminist Criminology _____

    C. Postmodern Criminology _____

D. Peacemaking Criminology _____
_____

V. Policy Implications _____
_____

DISCUSSION QUESTIONS

These discussion questions are found in the textbook at the end of the chapter. Your instructor may want to focus on these questions at the conclusion of the lecture on Chapter 9.

1. This book emphasizes a social problems versus social responsibility theme. Which of the theoretical perspectives discussed in this chapter (if any) support the social problems approach? Which (if any) support the social responsibility approach? Why?

2. Explain the difference between the consensus, pluralistic, and conflict perspectives. Which comes closest to your way of understanding society? Why?

3. What is Marxist criminology? How, if at all, does it differ from radical criminology? From critical criminology?

4. Does the Marxist perspective hold any significance for contemporary American society? Why or why not?

5. What are the fundamental propositions of feminist criminology? How would feminists change the study of crime?

6. What does it mean to say that traditional theories of crime need to be "deconstructed"? What role does deconstructionist thinking play in postmodern criminology?

STUDENT EXERCISES

Activity 1

Your instructor will divide the class into groups and assign your group one of the radical-critical theories discussed in this chapter. Develop a crime reduction and/or prevention policy that is based on this theory. Explain how the theory justifies the policy and why you expect the policy to reduce or prevent crime.

Activity 2

Locate a program in your community that emphasizes restorative justice (e.g., an alternative dispute resolution program). Describe the program and how it works to reintegrate offenders back into the community after they have been punished by the criminal justice system. Discuss the success/failure rate of the program.

CRIMINOLOGY TODAY ON THE WEB

http://www.critcrim.org

This is the Web site for the American Society of Criminology's Critical Criminology Division.

http://www.tryoung.com/journal-pomocrim/pomocrimindex.html

This is the Web site of the *Red Feather Journal of Postmodern Criminology*.

http://www.online.anu.edu.au/polsci/marx/marx.html

This site is devoted to Karl Marx and includes a considerable amount of information on Marxism.

http://www.westga.edu/~jfuller/peace.html

This site contains information on the peacemaking model of criminal justice.

http://www.restorativejustice.org

This site is devoted to the topic of restorative justice.

http://www.restorativejustice.org/rj2A_definition.htm

This page contains a detailed definition of restorative justice.

http://www.umsl.edu/~rkeel/200/powcontr.html

This Web site provides a discussion of power control and feminist theories.

PRACTICE QUESTIONS

True/False

_____ 1. The idea that communism would inevitably replace capitalism as the result of a natural historical process or dialetic was advanced by Karl Marx and Friedrich Engels.

_____ 2. The consensus perspective holds that the laws reflect the will of the interest group holding political and economic power.

_____ 3. The pluralistic perspective holds that conflict is a fundamental aspect of social life.

_____ 4. According to the pluralistic perspective, the legal system focuses primarily on the needs of the rich and politically powerful.

_____ 5. According to the conflict perspective, conflict between groups can be avoided through the use of the legal system.

_____ 6. Karl Marx believed that the natural outcome of the struggle between the proletariat and the bourgeoisie would be the overthrow of a communistic social order.

_____ 7. George Vold compared a criminal with a soldier, using crime to fight for the survival of his/her group.

_____ 8. Chambliss suggested that upper-class criminals are more likely to escape punishment by the criminal justice system because they are smarter and thus more capable of hiding their crimes.

_____ 9. Instrumental Marxism sees the criminal law and the criminal justice system as tools used to keep the poor disenfranchised.

_____ 10. Modern radical criminologists are calling for the abolition of capital punishment.

_____ 11. Left realism sees the criminal justice system and its agents as pawns of the powerful.

_____ 12. According to early feminist criminology, as gender equality increased, male and female criminality would take on similar characteristics.

_____ 13. Liberal feminists blame the present inequalities on the development within culture of separate spheres of influence and traditional attitudes about gender roles.

_____ 14. According to feminist criminologists, criminal laws reflect traditionally male ways of organizing the social world.

_____ 15. Semiotic criminology attempts to identify how language systems communicate values.

_____ 16. Adversarial court proceedings are based on the principle of participatory justice.

_____ 17. Peacemaking criminologists primarily envisions positive change on an individual level.

Fill in the Blank

18. The champion of the consensus perspective was _____.

Chapter 9 Sociological Theories III: Social Conflict

19. According to the conflict perspective, formal agencies of _____ coerce the unempowered to comply with the rules established by those in power.

20. The _____ are the capitalists, according to Marx.

21. George Vold described crime as the product of _____ conflict between groups.

22. According to Chambliss, _____ societies should reflect lower crime rates than capitalist societies.

23. According to _____ Marxists, the legal system keeps control in the hands of those who are already powerful.

24. Feminist criminology points out the inequities inherent in _____ forms of thought.

25. According to _____ theory, family class structure affects the social distribution of delinquency.

26. Anarchic criminology is a form of _____ criminology.

27. The _____ model of crime control focuses on effective ways for developing a shared consensus on critical issues that have the potential to seriously affect the quality of life.

28. _____ criminology emphasize practical applications of the principles of conflict resolution.

Multiple Choice

29. The idea that those who violate the law represent a unique subgroup with some distinguishing feature is a key principle of the _____ perspective.
    a. pluralist
    b. conflict
    c. consensus
    d. radical

30. The _____ perspective holds that conflict is a fundamental aspect of social life that can never be fully resolved.
    a. pluralistic
    b. conflict
    c. consensus
    d. radical

31. According to Karl Marx, the _____ are the exploited working class who are without power.
    a. proletariat
    b. bourgeoisie
    c. petit bourgeoisie
    d. materialists

32. Ralf Dahrendorf suggested that class conflicts arose over
    a. wealth.
    b. authority.
    c. race.
    d. crime.

33. According to _____, a spokesperson for modern radical thinkers, criminal behavior results from the coercive power of the state to enforce the will of the ruling class.
    a. Ralf Dahrendorf
    b. William Chambliss
    c. Harold Pepinsky
    d. Richard Quinney

34. Richard Quinney suggests that the problem of crime will only be solved by the creation of
    a. a class structure.
    b. a socialist society.
    c. hedonistic values.
    d. a capitalist society.

35. _____ criminology consists of a proactive call for change in the social conditions leading to crime, whereas _____ criminology is a way of critiquing social relationships leading to crime.
    a. Critical; radical
    b. Radical; critical
    c. Radical; pluralistic
    d. Critical; pluralistic

36. Modern radical criminologists have escalated their demands for
    a. an end to police misconduct.
    b. increased use of capital punishment.
    c. mandatory sentencing guidelines.
    d. increased funding for new prison construction.

37. _____ was an early feminist criminologist.
    a. Meda Chesney-Lind
    b. Rita Simon
    c. Kathleen Daly
    d. John Hagan

38. A demand for elimination of the traditional divisions of power and labor between the sexes would probably come from a(n) _____ feminist.
    a. socialist
    b. radical
    c. liberal
    d. alternative (women of color)

39. Stuart Henry and Dragan Milovanovic are known for their development of _____ criminology.
    a. constitutive
    b. anarchic
    c. peacemaking
    d. semiotic

40. A peace model is based on
    a. cooperation.
    b. retribution.
    c. just deserts.
    d. all of the above

Chapter 9 Sociological Theories III: Social Conflict

WORD SEARCH PUZZLE

Adler
Bourgeoisie
Chambliss
Critical
Feminist
Patriarchy
Peacemaking

Postmodern
Proletariat
Quinney
Radical
Vold
Young

```
N P A T R I A R C H Y V Y B
P R O L E T A R I A T P Y O
R E E Y R A D I C A L E T U
V D T D O L Q H V A D L E R
R N T U O U A J C W M P J G
K N S V I M N I G U F O X E
C V I N B K T G K Z D I Q O
T S N L M I G S C L C V B I
U E I Z R X V D O X Y Z D S
Y S M C Q O N D B P S X R I
S P E A C E M A K I N G S E
V W F V Q D F X T W D C F T
```

CROSSWORD PUZZLE

Across

4. A model suggesting that society generally agrees on what is right and wrong.
5. In Maxian theory, the working class.
6. A single-sex perspective, such as criminologists who study only the criminality of males.
9. He developed power control theory.
10. The author of *The Communist Manifesto*.
11. The tradition of male dominance.
12. Richard _____ is one of the most influential modern Marxists.

Down

1. The class of people that own the means of production.
2. Distinctions made between individuals based on important defining social characteristics.
3. _____ Marxism sees the criminal law as tools used by the powerful to control the poor.
7. _____ justice is a postmodern perspective stressing remedies over prison and punishment.
8. _____ feminists suggest that eliminating male domination should reduce crime rates for women.

crimes against persons

Learning Objectives

After reading this chapter, you should be able to:

1. Describe typologies of violent crime
2. Understand the key issues in explaining patterns of homicide
3. Understand the key issues in explaining patterns of violent crime
4. Explain why the context of familial assault is so important
5. Explain the major patterns of stalking
6. Identify the major characteristics of terrorism

CHAPTER SUMMARY

This chapter discusses various types of violent crime in the United States, including homicide, rape, robbery, assault, stalking, and terrorism. Homicide research focuses on two main theoretical frameworks, using subcultural and structural explanations to understand variations in homicide offending. Examinations of the relationship between the victim and the offender have found that homicides frequently involve family members, friends, or acquaintances. Victim precipitation studies characteristics of victims which may have precipitated their victimization, although the focus is not on "blaming the victim" for the crime. Factors such as weapons availability and the use of alcohol and drugs may also be associated with homicide. Gang membership may influence homicides; research shows several differences between homicides involving gang and nongang members. Serial and mass murder are also discussed, and several typologies are presented

It is difficult to measure the extent of rape in this country because the figures vary depending on the source used. Because many rapes are not reported to the police, official statistics frequently underestimate the extent of rape in the Untied States today. Rape myths, false assumptions about rape, contribute to underreporting of this crime. The common law definition of rape did not recognize male victims or rape within marriage; common law rules of evidence required victims to demonstrate physical resistance and to have some form of corroboration that the rape occurred. Rape law reform is designed to make the legal understanding of rape similar to that of other violent crime. All states have made significant changes in the common law crime of rape, although the impact of these reforms varies widely. The majority of rapes involve victims and offenders who are acquainted. College and university campuses typically have a high incidence of rape. Law reform has eliminated the marital exemption for rape, and the text presents a typology of men who rape their wives. Same-sex rape is common in both male and female correctional institutions, although the patterns vary. Rape within female prisons involves primarily the attack of inmates by male staff, whereas in male prisons the assault involves only inmates. Theoretical perspectives surrounding rape include feminist perspectives, the psychopathological perspective, Baron and Strauss's integrated theory of rape, and evolutionary and biological perspectives. Various typologies of rapists have been developed, often based on offender motivation

Robbery is considered a violent crime because the use or threat of force is involved in the crime. There is a high potential for injury and even death for robbery victims. Most robbers are generalists; few specialize in robbery alone. Many robbers are motivated by direct financial need. Offenders specializing in street robbery frequently target other criminals, especially lower-level drug dealers, both because of the opportunity to obtain not only money but also drugs and because these victims would be less likely to report their victimization to the police. With the exception of rape, robbery may be the most gender-differentiated serious crime in the United States as the vast majority of offenders are male. Male and female offenders differ significantly in how they carry out street robberies, although the primary motivation for both is economic.

Assault is the most frequent violent crime and is similar psychologically, although not legally, to homicide. The offender profiles for homicide and assault are extremely similar. The majority of assaults involve victims and offenders who are known to each other, frequently in a familial or intimate relationship. Research into familial violence has been hindered by the belief that the family is a private institution. NIBRS data on family assaults show some differences from aggravated assaults generally. Intimate partner assault involves assaultive behavior between persons involved in an intimate relationship. The majority of victims are female, although men may also be victims.

Stalking involves ongoing patterns of behavior that cause victims to fear for their personal safety. All states, and the federal government, currently have antistalking laws. Stalking behaviors can include making telephone calls, following the victim, sending letters, making threats, vandalizing property, or watching the victim. Data on the extent of stalking are available from the National Violence Against Women Survey. The majority of victims are women,

Chapter 10 Crime against Persons

and the majority of stalkers are men. Women are more likely to be stalked by an intimate partner, whereas men are more likely to be stalked by strangers or acquaintances. Cyberstalking involves using electronic communication such as e-mail or the Internet to harass individuals.

Terrorism is defined as "a violent act or an act dangerous to human life in violation of the criminal laws of the United States or of any state to intimidate or coerce a government, the civilian population, or any segment thereof, in furtherance of political or social objectives." Terrorist acts are distinguished from other violent crimes by the political motivation or ideology of the offender. The United States has to deal with both international terrorism, such as the 1983 bombing of the World Trade Center in New York City, and domestic terrorism, such as the 1995 Oklahoma City bombing. U.S. counterterrorist strategy involves a no-concession policy, the continued application of pressure to state sponsors of terrorism, and the application of the rule of law to international terrorists.

KEY CONCEPTS

acquaintance rape Rape characterized by a prior social, though not necessarily intimate or familial, relationship between the victim and the perpetrator.

crime typology A classification of crimes along a particular dimension, such as legal categories, offender motivation, victim behavior, or the characteristics of individual offenders.

cyberstalking An array of activities in which an offender may engage to harass or "follow" individuals, including e-mail and the Internet.

exposure-reduction theory A theory of intimate homicide which claims that a decline in domesticity, accompanied by an improvement in the economic status of women and a growth in domestic violence resources, explains observed decreases in intimate-partner homicide.

expressive crime A criminal offense that results from acts of interpersonal hostility, such as jealousy, revenge, romantic triangles, and quarrels.

institutional robbery Robbery that occurs in commercial settings, such as convenience stores, gas stations, and banks.

instrumental crime A goal-directed offense that involves some degree of planning by the offender.

intimate-partner assault A gender-neutral term used to characterize assaultive behavior that takes place between individuals involved in an intimate relationship.

National Violence against Women (NVAW) Survey A national survey of the extent and nature of violence against women conducted between November 1995 and May 1996 and funded through grants from the National Institute of Justice and the U.S. Department of Health and Human Services' National Center for Injury Prevention and Control.

nonprimary homicide Murder which involves victims and offenders who have no prior relationship and which usually occurs during the course of another crime such as robbery.

personal robbery Robbery that occurs on the highway or street or in a public place (and which is often referred to as "mugging") and robbery that occurs in residences.

primary homicide Murder involving family members, friends, and acquaintances.

rape myths A false assumption about rape such as, "When a woman says no, she really means yes." Rape myths characterize much of the discourse surrounding sexual violence.

rape shield law A statute providing for the protection of rape victims by ensuring that defendants do not introduce irrelevant facts about the victim's sexual history into evidence.

selective disinhibition A loss of self-control due to the characteristics of the social setting, drugs, alcohol, or a combination of both.

separation assault Violence inflicted by partners on significant others who attempt to leave an intimate relationship.

sibling offense An offense or incident that culminates in homicide. The offense or incident may be a crime, such as robbery, or an incident that meets a less stringent criminal definition, such as a lover's quarrel involving assault or battery.

spousal rape The rape of one spouse by the other. The term usually refers to the rape of a woman by her husband.

stalking A course of conduct directed at a specific person that involves repeated visual or physical proximity; nonconsensual communication; verbal, written, or implied threats; or a combination thereof, which would cause a reasonable person fear.

terrorism A violent act or an act dangerous to human life in violation of the criminal laws of the United States or of any state to intimidate or coerce a government, the civilian population, or any segment thereof, in furtherance of political or social objectives.[1]

victim precipitation Contributions made by the victim to the criminal event, especially those that led to its initiation.

Violence against Women Act (VAWA) A federal law enacted as a component of the 1994 Violent Crime Control and Law Enforcement Act and which was intended to address concerns about violence against women. The law focused on improving the interstate enforcement of protection orders, providing effective training for court personnel involved with women's issues, improving the training and collaboration of police and prosecutors with victim service providers, strengthening law enforcement efforts to reduce violence against women, and on efforts to increase services to victims of violence. President Clinton signed the reauthorization of this legislation, known as the Violence against Women Act 2000, into law on October 28, 2000. (10; 15)

Violent Criminal Apprehension Program (VICAP) Program of the Federal Bureau of Investigation focusing on serial murder investigation and the apprehension of serial killers.

CHAPTER OUTLINE

I. Introduction _____

_____

II. Violent Crime Typologies _____

_____

III. Homicide _____

_____

---

[1] Federal Bureau of Investigation, Counterterrorism Section, *Terrorism in the United States, 1987* (Washington, D.C.: FBI, December 1987).

Chapter 10 Crime against Persons

       A. The Subculture of Violence Thesis and Structural Explanations _____
   _____

       B. The Victim–Offender Relationship _____
   _____

       C. Instrumental and Expressive Violence _____
   _____

       D. Victim Precipitation _____
   _____

       E. Weapon Use _____
   _____

       F. Alcohol and Drug Use _____
   _____

       G. Gangs _____
   _____

       H. Serial Murder _____
   _____

       I. Mass Murder _____
   _____

IV. Rape _____
   _____

       A. Rape Myths _____
   _____

       B. The Common Law Definition of Rape _____
   _____

       C. Rape Law Reform _____
   _____

       D. The Social Context of Rape _____
   _____

       E. Theoretical Perspectives on Rape _____
   _____

       F. Typologies of Rapists _____
   _____

V. Robbery _____
   _____

       A. The Lethal Potential of Robbery _____
   _____

B. Criminal Careers of Robbers _____
_____

C. Robbery and Public Transportation _____
_____

D. The Motivation of Robbers _____
_____

E. Drug Robberies _____
_____

F. The Gendered Nature of Robbery _____
_____

VI. Assault _____
_____

A. Stranger Assault _____
_____

B. Assault within Families _____
_____

VII. Stalking _____
_____

A. The Extent of Stalking _____
_____

B. Victim-Offender Relationships in Stalking _____
_____

C. Stalking in Intimate-Partner Relationships _____
_____

D. Consequences of Stalking _____
_____

E. Cyberstalking _____
_____

VIII. Terrorism _____
_____

A. Countering the Terrorist Threat _____
_____

Chapter 10 Crime against Persons

DISCUSSION QUESTIONS

These discussion questions are found in the textbook at the end of the chapter. Your instructor may want to focus on these questions at the conclusion of the lecture on Chapter 10.

1. Why are crime typologies useful for understanding violent crime patterns?

2. What are the most common forms of violent crime? What characterizes these types of crimes?

3. What are the least common forms of violent crime? What characterizes these types of crimes?

4. Why was rape law reform necessary? What have been the beneficial aspects of this reform for rape victims?

5. Is robbery primarily a rational activity? Why or why not?

STUDENT EXERCISES

Activity 1

Recent legislation requires that universities publish statistics on crime on campus. Obtain information about violent crime occurring at your university campus. Compare the rates of serious violent crimes on campus to the rates in neighboring jurisdictions. How safe does your university appear to be?

Activity 2

Locate programs and other resources that are available on your university campus for victims of domestic violence and/or stalking. Bring these materials into class for discussion.

Activity 3

Obtain NCVS and UCR data on murder and aggravated assault and compare and contrast the two crimes. What are the similarities, and what are the differences between them? Consider factors such as the characteristics of the offenders and the victims, characteristics of the event (location, weapon used, when the crime occurred, etc.), and arrest and clearance rates.

Activity 4

Select three theories that you have discussed in previous chapters and discuss how each of these might explain the crimes of assault and robbery.

CRIMINOLOGY TODAY ON THE WEB

http://www.icpsr.umich.edu/NACJD/HRWG

This is the home page of the Homicide Research Working Group, organized by the American Society of Criminology in 1991.

http://www.cs.utk.edu/~bartley/acquaint/acquaintRape.html

This Web site provides an article on date and acquaintance rape.

http://www.pbs.org/kued/nosafeplace

This Web site provides a link to a 1998 PBS program discussing violence against women. This site includes the program script, links and other resources, and other material.

http://www.asksam.com/cavnet
http://www.cavnet2.org

These Web sites provide links to CAVNET, the Communities Against Violence Network, which addresses domestic violence, sexual assault, rape, stalking, and other types of violent crime.

http://www.ojp.usdoj.gov/nij/pubs-sum/181867.htm

This Web site provides a link to results from the National Violence Against Women Survey, which asked respondents about their experiences as victims of various types of intimate-partner violence, including rape, assault, and stalking.

http://www.ojp.usdoj.gov/vawo

This is the home page of the U.S. Department of Justice Violence Against Women Office.

http://www.usdoj.gov/criminal/cybercrime/cyberstalking.htm

This site makes available the 1999 Attorney General's report on cyberstalking.

Chapter 10 Crime against Persons

http://www.antistalking.com
This is the antistalking Web site.

http://www.pbs.org/wgbh/nova/bombing/index.html
This Web site provides a link to a PBS program on the bombing of America, including coverage of the Unabomber case.

http://www.fbi.gov/ucr/hatecm.htm
This site makes available hate crime statistics published by the FBI.

http://www.terrorism.com/index.shtml
This is the home page of the Terrorism Research Center.

PRACTICE QUESTIONS

True/False

_____ 1. Murder for profit is a typical homicide.

_____ 2. Evidence suggests that the South differs from other regions in terms of the frequency of homicide.

_____ 3. A homicide that occurs during an incident that began as a robbery is an example of an instrumental homicide.

_____ 4. According to the availability factor, access to guns may increase their presence in all types of interactions, not just criminal interactions.

_____ 5. Serial killers generally use a standard pattern of offending and method of killing.

_____ 6. Most serial killers are psychotic.

_____ 7. Female serial killers follow a pattern similar to that of male serialists.

_____ 8. VICAP is primarily a tool for detecting offenders.

_____ 9. Mass murderers are more difficult to apprehend than serial killers.

_____ 10. Rape law reforms have eliminated the requirement that the victim physically resist the attacker.

_____ 11. Rape law reform involved creation of the marital exemption for rape.

_____ 12. Anger rapes generally involve no prior planning on the part of the offender.

_____ 13. Supremacy rapists are more interested in the punishment given to the victim than to the sexual contact, according to Dennis Stevens.

14. Institutional robberies occur in commercial settings.

_____ 15. Street robbers frequently target drug dealers.

_____ 16. Most aggravated assaults are spontaneous.

_____ 17. Men and women are equally likely to be victims of stalking.

Fill in the Blank

18. Gottfredson and Hirschi's general theory of crime is an example of a(n) _____ typology.

19. _____ homicides involve victims and offenders who have no prior relationship.

20. Victim-precipitated homicides are more likely to be committed by _____.

21. _____ murder involves killing at least four victims at one location within one event.

22. The most frequently occurring type of serial killer, according to the Fox and Levin typology, is the _____ killer.

23. According to FBI profiling theory, _____ killers have higher levels of intelligence and social skills.

24. _____ laws protect rape victims by ensuring that defendants do not introduce irrelevant facts of the victim's sexual past into evidence.

25. According to Groth, _____ rapists generally plan their crimes.

26. According to Dennis Stevens, _____ rapists are trying to regain some imaginary goal that had been part of their past.

27. _____ is the most frequently occurring violent crime.

28. _____ involves the use of electronic communication to harass individuals.

Multiple Choice

29. African-Americans are disproportionately represented in the homicide statistics as
    a. victims.
    b. offenders.
    c. both victims and offenders.
    d. neither victims nor offenders.

30. According to Williams and Flewelling, _____ is a stronger predictor of family homicide than of stranger homicide.
    a. percent poor
    b. population size
    c. the context of the event
    d. the victim–offender relationship

31. The _____ focuses on explaining the role that alcohol plays in homicide.
    a. general theory of crime
    b. subculture of violence thesis
    c. selective disinhibition theory
    d. critical criminological perspective

32. Reasonable estimates suggest that approximately _____ murders each year are the result of serial killings.
    a. 50
    b. 100
    c. 1000
    d. 5000

33. The _____ serial killer frequently plays a "cat and mouse" game with the victim before committing the murder.
    a. visionary
    b. comfort
    c. hedonistic
    d. power seeker

34. According to Levin and Fox's typology of mass murder, the most common motive for such a crime is
    a. revenge.
    b. love.
    c. profit.
    d. terror.

35. Which of the following was not required by the rules of evidence under the common law definition of rape?
    a. The victim had to demonstrate physical resistance to the act.
    b. The victim must have some form of corroboration that the rape occurred.
    c. The victim's previous sexual history could be admitted as relevant information.
    d. The victim had to be the spouse of the offender.

36. The integrated theory of rape was developed by
    a. Baron and Straus.
    b. Hirschi and Gottfredson.
    c. Thornhill and Palmer.
    d. Hazelwood and Burgess.

37. According to the Hazelwood and Burgess typology of rapists, the blitz approach is used by the _____ category of rapist.
    a. anger-excitation
    b. power-reassurance
    c. anger-retaliatory
    d. power-assertive

38. Which of the following types of robbery is most likely to be affected by crime prevention strategies?
    a. Muggings
    b. Robberies of commercial establishments
    c. Robberies on mass transit
    d. Personal robberies

39. Which of the following is a characteristic of female robbers?
    a. They almost always use guns.
    b. They target victims involved in street life.
    c. They frequently rob females in a physically confrontational manner.
    d. They have one clear style of robbery.

40. Stalking behaviors include
    a. following the victim.
    b. making phone calls.
    c. vandalizing property.
    d. all of the above

WORD SEARCH PUZZLE

- Acquaintance
- Cyberstalking
- Fox
- Horney
- Nonprimary
- Robbery
- Spousal rape
- Stalking
- Straus
- Terrorism
- Typology
- VICAP

```
C K S D B E M A N Y F C C T E
Z U G Y B Y G O L O P Y T I R
T H M N S S E Q X G B J C I N
B A S O T K F N Q E Y P R S C
E C C Y R A M I R P N O N S S
B P I Q A K K S J O B Q I K L
Z Y A U U Q T E I B H E Z W L
F T N R S A G E E R M B Q B I
Z O L P L X I R M U O D S U J
T O N K J A Y N Q T Q R C V O
Q U I O M R S N T B O Q R Z I
T N M E C E J U L A O P Q E Z
G B H F G Q Z X O U N N L L T
A L F L O X V S Q P A C I V X
D D W I J S U Y F X S I E L H
```

Chapter 10 Crime against Persons

CROSSWORD PUZZLE

Across

1. Victim _____ includes contributions made by the victim to the criminal event.
4. A(n) _____ crime results from acts of interpersonal hostility such as jealousy or revenge.
6. An array of activities using the Internet or e-mail to harass people.
8. Behaviors directed at a specific person that would cause a reasonable person fear.
9. Violent acts intended to coerce a government for political or social objectives.
10. A(n) _____ offense is one that culminates in homicide.

Down

2. Robbery of a gas station is an example of _____ robbery.
3. A crime _____ classifies crimes along a particular dimension such as legal categories.
5. A(n) _____ crime is a goal-directed offense involving some degree of planning by the offender.
7. Mugging is an example of _____ robbery.

crimes against property

Learning Objectives

After reading this chapter, you should be able to:

1. Understand the distinction between professional criminals and other kinds of property offenders
2. Identify the major forms of property crime
3. Explain the rationalizations and motivations characteristic of property offenders
4. Understand the application of various typologies to property offenses
5. Describe how stolen goods are distributed

CHAPTER SUMMARY

This chapter discusses various types of property crime in the United States, including larceny/theft, burglary, stolen property, and arson. The difference between persistent thieves and professional criminals is examined briefly. Professional offenders commit crime with some skill, make a living from crime, and spend relatively little time incarcerated. Persistent thieves are those who continue in common law property crimes despite having at best an ordinary level of success. Most property offenders do not specialize in one type of crime. The issue of property crimes as rational choice is also discussed.

Larceny/theft, which does not involve the use of force or illegal entry, is the most frequently occurring property crime, with theft from a motor vehicle being the largest category. Theft on college campuses is influenced by the size and design of the campus. Motor vehicle theft can include a variety of means of transportation, but automobiles are the vehicle most commonly stolen. It is the crime where the largest percentage of victims miss time from work as a result of the crime. Most completed motor vehicle thefts are reported to the police. Theft of external car parts may be committed for a variety of reasons; theft from motor vehicles also includes taking items from within the vehicle (stereo equipment, cameras, briefcases, etc.) Joyriding involves opportunistic car theft committed by groups of teenagers for fun or thrills; the preferred vehicle is an American-made sports car. Jockeys are professional car thieves who are regularly involved in steal-to-order jobs; they are rarer but represent the most costly and serious form of auto theft.

Employee theft and shoplifting are both increasing. Employee theft costs retailers more than customer shoplifting and is often perceived as more serious. Historically, shoplifting was pervasive among middle-class women. Today, it is a crime that crosses class lines and is not committed primarily by women; juveniles are overrepresented in current statistics on offending. Research suggests that shoplifting is one of the largest categories of unofficial delinquency and may be a gateway offense leading to more serious and chronic types of offending. Various typologies of shoplifters are discussed.

Burglary is usually a victim-avoiding crime; offenders prefer to avoid direct confrontation with their victims. Burglary is more common in large metropolitan areas and in the Midwest. Changes in routine activities since World War II may help explain changes in burglary rates. A typology of burglars is discussed. The primary motivation for burglary is the need for fast cash, often to maintain the offender's street status or to support a party lifestyle. Commercial targets are selected based on their suitability, with retail establishments being the most common choice. Residential burglars rarely target homes of family or friends but may target homes of people otherwise known to them. Other key elements in target selection include a reluctance to burglarize occupied dwellings, residences with complex security devices, and residences with a dog that could make noise or injure the offender. The recent increase in robbery and decrease in burglary may be linked to the increased demand for crack cocaine. Some burglaries have sexual motivations, such as voyeuristic or fetish burglaries; there may also be a link between burglary and later sexual offending.

Receiving stolen property involves three key elements: buying and selling, stolen property, and knowing property to be stolen. The fence is a middleman who takes on the role of moving stolen goods from the professional thief to the customer; most thieves do not use a professional fence to dispose of stolen goods. Paul Cromwell's typology of criminal receivers is discussed.

The FBI records an incident as an arson only after it has been investigated and officially classified as arson by the proper investigative authorities; fires of suspicious or unknown origin are not included in the FBI's arson statistics. The recent wave of church arsons in the United States and the motivations behind these crimes are discussed. Arson for profit is fairly rare; the majority of those involved in arson are juveniles.

Chapter 11 Crimes against Property

KEY CONCEPTS

booster A frequent shoplifter.

fence An individual or group involved in the buying, selling, and distribution of stolen goods. Also called *criminal receiver*.

gateway offense An offense, usually fairly minor in nature, that leads to more serious offenses. Shoplifting, for example, may be a gateway offense to more serious property crimes.

jockey A professional car thief involved regularly in calculated, steal-to-order car thefts.

joyriding An opportunistic car theft, often committed by a teenager seeking fun or thrills.

occasional offender A criminal offender whose offending patterns are guided primarily by opportunity.

offense specialization A preference for engaging in a certain type of offense to the exclusion of others.

persistent thief One who continues in common-law property crimes despite no better than an ordinary level of success.

professional criminal A criminal offender who makes a living from criminal pursuits, is recognized by other offenders as professional, and engages in offending that is planned and calculated.

snitch An amateur shoplifter.

CHAPTER OUTLINE

I. Introduction _____

II. Persistent and Professional Thieves _____

    A. Criminal Careers of Property Offenders _____

    B. Property Offenders and Rational Choice _____

III. Larceny/Theft _____

    A. Prevalence and Profile of Larceny/Theft _____

    B. Theft on College Campuses _____

    C. Motor Vehicle Theft _____

D. Shoplifting and Employee Theft _____
_____

IV. Burglary _____
_____

   A. The Social Ecology of Burglary _____
_____

   B. Types of Burglars _____
_____

   C. Burglary Locales _____
_____

   D. The Motivation of Burglars _____
_____

   E. Target Selection _____
_____

   F. Costs of Burglary _____
_____

   G. The Burglary-Drug Connection _____
_____

   H. The Sexualized Context of Burglary _____
_____

V. Stolen Property _____
_____

   A. The Role of Criminal Receivers _____
_____

VI. Arson _____
_____

   A. Fire Setters _____
_____

DISCUSSION QUESTIONS

These discussion questions are found in the textbook at the end of the chapter. Your instructor may want to focus on these questions at the conclusion of the lecture on Chapter 11.

1. Explain the differences between professional property offenders and persistent property offenders.

Chapter 11   Crimes against Property

2. To what extent are property offenders rational actors? Use examples from larceny, burglary, and receiving stolen property to illustrate your points.

3. Why is so much attention given to shoplifting among adolescents?

4. How are drugs involved in the offending patterns of burglars?

5. What does it mean to talk about the "sexualized context" of burglary?

6. How are "honest" citizens and professional criminal receivers connected?

7. To what extent is "thrill seeking" a motivation behind several types of property offenses?

STUDENT EXERCISES

Activity 1

Recent legislation requires that universities publish statistics on crime on campus. Obtain information about property crime occurring at your university campus. Compare the rates of property crime on campus to the rates in neighboring jurisdictions. How safe does your university appear to be?

Activity 2

Your instructor will divide the class into groups and assign each group to a building on campus (e.g., the university library, the student union, a dormitory). Examine this building and its occupants for vulnerability to property crime (burglary, theft, etc.) Develop at least three workable techniques for reducing the likelihood of property crime victimization for the occupants of this building.

CRIMINOLOGY TODAY ON THE WEB

http://www.ojp.usdoj.gov/bjs/cvict.htm

This site provides summary findings from the National Crime Victimization Survey. Click on the property crime chart for more information about property crime trends in the United States.

http://www.fbi.gov/hq/cid/arttheft/arttheft.htm

This is the Web site of the FBI's division specializing in art theft.

http://www.ojp.usdoj.gov/BJA/html/wyc.htm

This is a link to the Bureau of Justice Statistics' Watch Your Car program, a national voluntary motor vehicle theft prevention program established by the U.S. Attorney General.

http://www.ojp.usdoj.gov/bjs/glance/mvt.htm

This link provides information from the Bureau of Justice Statistics on the rates of motor vehicle theft in the United States.

http://www.telalink.net/~police/risk/index.htm

This Web site of the Metro Nashville Police Department includes a series of tests to determine your risk of victimization of various types of crimes, including burglary.

http://www.crime-freesecurity.com/crime.html

This Web site provides information on residential burglary and how to make your home more secure.

http://www.commpro.com/burglar/tips.html

This is the Bluff a Burglar Web site.

http://www.atf.treas.gov

This is the home page of the Bureau of Alcohol, Tobacco, and Firearms, which is the agency responsible for the investigation of arson of federal buildings.

http://www.usfa.fema.gov/napi

This is the U.S. Fire Administration's arson prevention page.

PRACTICE QUESTIONS

True/False

_____ 1. Professional criminals are rare in the world of theft.

_____ 2. Larceny involves the use of force.

_____ 3. The Crime Awareness and Campus Security Act of 1990 requires universities to make public data on thefts occurring on campus.

_____ 4. The largest percentage of stolen vehicles are taken from a parking lot or garage.

_____ 5. Police are less able to identify stolen car parts than stolen vehicles.

_____ 6. Cars stolen by jockeys are most likely to be recovered by the police.

_____ 7. Today, shoplifting is committed primarily by women.

_____ 8. Boosters primarily keep the items they shoplift.

_____ 9. The majority of burglars are professionals.

Chapter 11 Crimes against Property 139

____ 10. Burglary rates are higher in rural areas.

____ 11. Residential burglary that occurs at night is considered to be more serious.

____ 12. That pattern of victim–offender relationship found in property crimes is different from that found in violent crimes.

____ 13. Burglary targets are rarely chosen on the spur of the moment.

____ 14. Property crimes may have more of an effect than violent crimes on a victim's decision to move.

____ 15. Research suggests that there may be a link between burglary and sexual offenses.

____ 16. Fires that are of suspicious or unknown origin are classified by the FBI as arson.

____ 17. Adults are more likely than juveniles to be involved in commercial arson.

Fill in the Blank

18. A(n) _____ continues in common law property crimes despite having an ordinary level of success, at best.

19. _____ are the most commonly stolen vehicles.

20. A car thief who is regularly involved in stealing cars to order is a(n) _____.

21. In Finland, shoplifting is most prevalent among _____.

22. According to Richard Moore's typology of shoplifters, _____ shoplifters are inexperienced, rarely plan the crime in advance, and are remorseful when apprehended.

23. According to victimization data, approximately _____ percent of households in the United States will be burglarized at least once over an average lifetime.

24. According to Mike Maguire's typology of burglars, _____ burglars are professionals.

25. Commercial burglary locations are usually selected based on the _____ of the target.

26. _____ burglaries occur when the offender steals particular items because they provide an outlet for sexual gratification.

27. A _____ fence is one whose illicit lines of goods are distinct from those of legitimate commerce.

Multiple Choice

28. Malcolm Kline used the term _____ to refer to the heterogeneous and unplanned nature of offending found among gang members.
    a. professional criminal activity
    b. offense specialization
    c. cafeteria-style offending
    d. persistent offending

29. The most frequent type of larceny, according to the UCR, is
    a. shoplifting.
    b. theft from a motor vehicle.
    c. theft from a building.
    d. purse snatching.

30. Which of the following cars is most likely to be preferred by car thieves?
    a. Toyota Camry
    b. Ford Taurus
    c. Dodge Intrepid
    d. Mitsubishi Gallant

31. The most costly form of auto theft is
    a. joyriding.
    b. professional theft.
    c. theft for use in a crime.
    d. stripping.

32. Today, _____ are overrepresented in offense statistics on shoplifting.
    a. juveniles
    b. young adults
    c. senior citizens
    d. middle-class women

33. According to Richard Moore's typology of shoplifters, _____ shoplifters generally had psychological problems.
    a. impulsive
    b. episodic
    c. amateur
    d. occasional

34. According to McShane and Noonan's typology of shoplifters, the _____ category includes persons who are older, with higher levels of education than other groups, and more likely to be married and male.
    a. rebel
    b. enigma
    c. reactionary
    d. infirm

35. According to UCR data, the most common type of burglary involves _____ entry.
    a. forcible
    b. attempted forcible
    c. unlawful
    d. lawful

36. According to Mike Maguire's typology of burglars, juveniles committing crimes on the spur of the moment fall into the category of _____ burglars.
    a. high-level
    b. midrange
    c. low-level
    d. multilevel

37. The most common commercial establishment to be targeted for burglary is a _____ establishment.
    a. wholesale
    b. retail
    c. service
    d. banking

Chapter 11 Crimes against Property

38. Which of the following is not an element considered when selecting a target for a burglary?
    a. Whether the residence has a security device
    b. Whether a dog lives in the residence
    c. Whether the residence is unoccupied
    d. They are all elements considered by the offender when selecting a target.

39. According to Cromwell's typology of criminal receivers, the _____ receiver is most likely to be used by high-level burglars.
    a. professional
    b. avocational
    c. amateur
    d. episodic

40. According to Cromwell's typology of criminal receivers, _____ receivers generally buy stolen property primarily for personal consumption.
    a. professional
    b. avocational
    c. amateur
    d. episodic

WORD SEARCH PUZZLE

Booster
Fence
Gateway
Jockey
Joyrider
Klockers

Persistent
Professional
Shover
Snitch
Steffensmeier

```
S G U P C Y A W E T A G O I K
W T B R M X L S N I T C H L N
O Y E O G R R E D I R Y O J M
L J D F O N T M D J O C K E Y
E C N E F S E V D A K R F Y Y
B O L S I E T O Z E M S S W I
D P E S Q M N E R D W P K M I
E B R I K C D S R S U O U V P
R E V O H S X H M L S E B H R
P N M N P R N S A E F G Q U T
W H T A C T X Q P R I T D U W
F Q X L E C H B I X X E I F D
J E I R T H O I P X C F R Z X
```

Chapter 11 Crimes against Property

CROSSWORD PUZZLE

Across
1. A frequent shoplifter.
5. A _____ criminal makes a living from crime.
9. An opportunistic car theft, often committed by a teenager seeking fun or thrills.

Down
2. Offense _____ involves a preference for committing a certain type of crime.
3. A professional car thief involved in steal-to-order car thefts.
4. Shoplifting may be a _____ offense to more serious property crimes.
5. A _____ Thief continues in property crimes despite no better than an ordinary level of success.
6. An offender whose patterns of offending are guided primarily by opportunity.
7. An amateur shoplifter.
8. A criminal receiver.

white-collar and organized crime

CHAPTER 12

Learning Objectives

After reading this chapter, you should be able to:

1. Discuss white-collar crime and its etiology
2. Describe the nature of corporate crime
3. Explain the history of organized crime in the United States, including La Costa Nostra
4. Identify new and emerging organized criminal groups within the United States
5. Discuss the relationship between organized crime and the law

CHAPTER SUMMARY

This chapter reviews two specific categories of crime: white-collar crime and organized crime. Edwin Sutherland's original 1939 definition of white-collar crime focused on the social standing of the offender; today, the focus has shifted to the type of offense committed. Currently, one commonly used term is *occupational crime*, which includes any criminal act committed through opportunities created in the course of a legal occupation. Gary S. Green developed a typology of occupational crime which includes four categories: organizational occupational crime, state authority occupational crime, professional occupational crime, and individual occupational crime. Corporate crime, another form of white-collar crime, is committed for the benefit of the corporation rather than the individual employee. One new area of corporate crime is environmental crime. There have been a number of attempts to explain white-collar crime. Sutherland applied elements of differential association theory to white-collar crime. Travis Hirschi and Michael Gottfredson stated that white-collar criminals are motivated by the same forces that drive other offenders and suggest that a general theory of crime can explain white-collar crime and other forms of crime as well. John Braithwaite states that white-collar criminals are motivated by a disparity between corporate goals and legitimate means and suggests that business subcultures encourage illegal behavior. Dealing with white-collar crime may require ethical, enforcement, structural, and political reforms.

Criminal societies such as La Cosa Nostra and the Mafia began in Italy several centuries ago and migrated to the United States during a period of Italian immigration during the late 1800s. Prohibition, which began after the passage of the eighteenth Amendment to the U.S. Constitution in 1919, established the wealth and power of modern organized crime syndicates and effectively institutionalized official corruption. The Wickersham Commission specifically mentioned the corrupting influence that Prohibition was having on professional law enforcement in the United States. During this period, organized crime leaders also worked to consolidate power. The repeal of the Eighteenth Amendment in 1933 ended Prohibition. Organized crime activities went underground for the next twenty years. National attention was again focused on organized crime in 1951, when the federal Kefauver Committee reported that a nationwide crime syndicate was operating in many large U.S. cities. Eventually, federal investigations established the existence of twenty-four crime families operating in the United States under the direction of a commission.

Organized crime activities include racketeering, vice, theft/fence rings, gangs, and terrorism. The primary motivation for all organized crime activities is money. Members of organized Sicilian-American criminal groups are governed by a strict code of conduct known as *omerta*, which functions to concentrate power in the hands of the crime bosses as well as ensuring their protection. The two key requirements imposed by the code are to obey one's superiors and to keep silent; the penalty for failing to adhere to these rules is death. Transnational organized crime involves unlawful activity undertaken and supported by organized criminal groups operating across national boundaries; it is becoming a key challenge to law enforcement agencies. The most important piece of federal legislation ever passed to target organized crime activities is RICO, which includes a provision for asset forfeiture, making it possible for federal officials to seize all proceeds of persons involved in racketeering. Organized crime is difficult to control; the text discusses various approaches to the control of organized criminal activity.

KEY CONCEPTS

asset forfeiture The authorized seizure of money, negotiable instruments, securities, or other things of value. In federal antidrug laws; the authorization of judicial representatives to seize all monies, negotiable instruments, securities, or other things of value furnished or intended to be furnished by any person in exchange for a controlled substance, and all proceeds traceable to such an exchange.

Chapter 12 White-Collar and Organized Crime

corporate crime A violation of a criminal statute either by a corporate entity or by its executives, employees, or agents acting on behalf of and for the benefit of the corporation, partnership, or other form of business entity.[1]

Cosa Nostra Literally, "our thing." A criminal organization of Sicilian origin. Also call *the Mafia, the Outfit, the Mob, the syndicate*, or simply *the organization*.

designer drugs One of the "new substances designed by slightly altering the chemical make-up of other illegal or tightly controlled drugs."[2]

environmental crimes A violation of the criminal law which, although typically committed by businesses or by business officials, may also be committed by other people or by organizational entities and which damages some protected or otherwise significant aspect of the natural environment.

ethnic succession The continuing process whereby one immigrant or ethnic group succeeds another by assuming its position in society.

Kefauver Committee The popular name for the federal Special Committee to Investigate Originated Crime in Interstate Commerce, formed in 1951.

money laundering The process of converting illegally earned assets, originating as cash, to one or more alternative forms to conceal such incriminating factors as illegal origin and true ownership.[3]

occupational crime Any act punishable by law which is committed through opportunity created in the course of an occupation that is legal.[4]

omerta The informal, unwritten code of organized crime which demands silence and loyalty, among other things, of family members.

organized crime The unlawful activities of the members of a highly organized, disciplined association engaged in supplying illegal goods and services, including gambling, prostitution, loan-sharking, narcotics, and labor racketeering.[5]

Racketeer Influenced and Corrupt Organizations (RICO) A statute which was part of the federal Organized Crime Control Act of 1970, and which is intended to combat criminal conspiracies.

state-organized crime Acts defined by law as criminal and committed by state officials in the pursuit of their work as representatives of the state.[6]

transnational organized crime Unlawful activity undertaken and supported by organized criminal groups operating across national boundaries.

white-collar crime Violations of the criminal law committed by a person of respectability and high social status in the course of his or her occupation.

---

1 Michael L. Benson, Francis T. Cullen, and William J. Maakestad, *Local Prosecutors and Corporate Crime* (Washington, D.C.: National Institute of Justice, 1993).
2 James A. Inciardi, *The War on Drugs II* (Mountain View, CA: Mayfield), 1992, p. 79.
3 Clifford Karchmer and Douglas Ruch, "State and Local Money Laundering Control Strategies," *NIJ Research in Brief* (Washington, D.C.: National Institute of Justice, 1992), p. 1.
4 Gary S. Green, *Occupational Crime* (Chicago: Nelson-Hall, 1990), p. 12.
5 The Omnibus Crime Control Act of 1970.
6 William J. Chambliss, "State-Organized Crime-The American Society of Criminology, 1988 Presidential Address," *Criminology*, Vol. 27, No. 2 (1989), pp. 183-208.

CHAPTER OUTLINE

I. Introduction

II. White-Collar Crime

    A. Definitional Evolution of White-Collar Crime

    B. Corporate Crime

    C. Causes of White-Collar Crime

    D. Dealing with White-Collar Crime

III. Organized Crime

    A. History of Organized Crime in the United States

    B. A Rose by Any Other Name—La Cosa Nostra

    C. Prohibition and Official Corruption

    D. The Centralization of Organized Crime

    E. La Cosa Nostra Today

    F. Activities of Organized Crime

    G. Code of Conduct

    H. Other Organized Criminal Groups

    I. Transnational Organized Crime

    J. Organized Crime and the Law

IV. Policy Issues: The Control of Organized Crime

Chapter 12 White-Collar and Organized Crime

DISCUSSION QUESTIONS

These discussion questions are found in the textbook at the end of the chapter. Your instructor may want to focus on these questions at the conclusion of the lecture on Chapter 12.

1. What is the difference between white-collar crime and organized crime? What linkages, if any, might exist between the two?

2. What types of white-collar crime has this chapter identified? Is corporate crime a form of white-collar crime? Is occupational crime a form of white-collar crime?

3. Describe a typical organized crime family, as outlined in this chapter. Why does a crime family contain so many different "levels"?

4. What is *money laundering*? How might money laundering be reduced or prevented? Can you think of any strategies this chapter does not discuss for the reduction of money laundering activities in the United States? If so, what are they?

5. What strategies does this chapter discuss for combating the activities of organized crime? Which seem best to you? Why? Can you think of any other strategies that might be effective? If so, what are they?

STUDENT EXERCISES

Activity 1

Explain how the routine activity approach to explaining crime might be applied to organized crime.

Activity 2

Obtain a chart showing the organizational structure of a modern legitimate corporation. Compare this to Figure 12-1, which shows the structure of a Mafia family. How do the structures differ? What similarities do you see?

CRIMINOLOGY TODAY ON THE WEB

http://www.usdoj.gov/atr
This is the home page of the U.S. Department of Justice Anti–Trust Division.

http://www.epa.gov
This is the home page for the Environmental Protection Agency.

http://www.occ.treas.gov/launder/orig1.htm
This Web site includes information on money laundering and discusses ways that banks can protect themselves becoming involved in money laundering schemes.

http://www.nw3c.org
This is the home page of the National White Collar Crime Center, which provides support services for law enforcement agencies that are involved in fighting economic crime.

http://www.wccfighter.com
This is the home page for "White Collar Crime Fighter," an online newsletter.

http://www4.law.cornell.edu/uscode/18/ch96.html
At this site, read Title 18, Chapter 96 of the U.S. Code, the Racketeer Influenced and Corrupt Organizations Act (RICO).

PRACTICE QUESTIONS

True/False

_____ 1. According to Sutherland, it is rare for large corporations to become involved in illegal activities until long after their inception.

_____ 2. In general, white-collar crime appears to be punished less severely than street crime.

_____ 3. According to Sutherland, white-collar criminality always involves a violation of the criminal law.

_____ 4. The Union Carbide Corporation liability case centered on the issue of criminal negligence.

_____ 5. Hirschi and Gottfredson have outlined a theory that is specific to white-collar crime.

_____ 6. Structural reforms to address white-collar crime may include adding members of the public to corporate boards.

_____ 7. During the last half-century, organized criminal activity has been dominated by the descendants of Irish-American immigrants.

_____ 8. The Unione Siciliana was an organization set up as a rival to the American Mafia.

_____ 9. One result of Prohibition was police corruption.

_____ 10. With a crime family, caporegime are the soldiers.

_____ 11. Organized crime families may infiltrate legitimate businesses for the purpose of money laundering.

_____ 12. The code of *omerta* functions to ensure the protection of crime bosses.

Chapter 12 White-Collar and Organized Crime

____ 13. One hallmark of a true criminal organization is that it has a continuity over time as personnel within the organization change.

____ 14. Many Russian private security firms are fronts for Russian gangsters and organized criminals.

____ 15. RICO made racketeering illegal.

____ 16. Federal statutes such as the Money Laundering Control Act have succeeded in reducing the problem of money laundering in the United States.

Fill in the Blank

17. Sutherland claimed that the only real difference between modern-day white-collar criminals and those of the past is that today they are more _____.

18. The early definition of white-collar crime focused on the _____.

19. _____ crime is a violation of a criminal statute by a corporate entity or by its executives, employees, or agents acting on behalf of and for the benefit of the corporation.

20. According to Hirschi and Gottfredson, the personal characteristics of most white-collar workers are those that would be expected to produce _____ in behavior.

21. Braithwaite has recommended the implementation of a(n) _____ model as a way of reducing white-collar offending.

22. The elimination of campaign contributions from businesses is an example of the _____ area of white-collar crime reform.

23. _____ refers to the continuing process by which one immigrant group supplants another through assumption of a particular place in society.

24. During Prohibition, organized crime leaders worked to _____ power.

25. The function of the _____ within a crime family is to collect information for the boss.

26. _____ involves lending money at rates significantly higher than legally prescribed limits.

27. The _____ Act made it a violation of federal law to engage in any criminal behavior that interferes with interstate commerce.

28. The federal Money Laundering Control Act requires banks to report to the government all currency transactions that exceed _____.

Multiple Choice

29. White-collar crime was originally defined by
    a. Emile Durkheim.
    b. Edwin Sutherland.
    c. Richard Quinney.
    d. George Vold.

30. Currently, the concept of white-collar crime focuses on
    a. the nature of the crime.
    b. the person involved.
    c. the occupation involved.
    d. the work environment.

31. According to Gary Green's typology of occupational crime, _____ occupational crimes benefit the employing agency.
    a. professional
    b. state authority
    c. organizational
    d. individual

32. _____ suggest(s) that white-collar criminals are motivated by the same forces that drive other criminals.
    a. Edwin Sutherland
    b. Travis Hirschi and Michael Gottfredson
    c. Gary Green and Gilbert Geis
    d. John Braithwaite

33. _____ occupational criminals are unlikely to be deterred by sanction or threat.
    a. Professional
    b. State authority
    c. Organizational
    d. Individual

34. Prior to the arrival of Italian immigrants, many of the rackets in New York City were run by _____ gangsters.
    a. Irish
    b. Jewish
    c. Hispanic
    d. Asian

35. Prohibition was repealed by passage of the _____ Amendment to the U.S. Constitution.
    a. Tenth
    b. Eighteenth
    c. Twenty-first
    d. Twenty-fourth

36. The *consigliere* is also known as the
    a. boss.
    b. underboss.
    c. counselor.
    d. lieutenant.

37. The strict unwritten code of conduct of organized crime, which demands silence and loyalty, is known as the
    a. Cosa Nostra.
    b. RICO.
    c. *omerta*.
    d. tong.

38. Unlawful activity undertaken and supported by organized criminal groups operating across national boundaries is known as _____ organized crime.
    a. international
    b. intercontinental
    c. transnational
    d. overseas

Chapter 12 White-Collar and Organized Crime

39. The single most important piece of federal legislation that specifically targets organized crime activities is
    a. omerta.
    b. RICO.
    c. the Hobbs Act.
    d. the United States Code.

40. Legalizing or decriminalizing illegal drugs falls into which of Howard Abadinsky's approaches to controlling organized crime?
    a. Increasing the risk of involvement in organized crime
    b. Increasing law enforcement authority
    c. Reducing the economic lure of involvement
    d. Decreasing opportunity for organized criminal activity

WORD SEARCH PUZZLE

- Braithwaite
- Corporate
- Cosa Nostra
- Environmental
- Geis
- Gottfredson
- Hirschi
- Kefauver
- Mafia
- Occupational
- Omerta
- RICO
- Succession
- Sutherland
- Transnational
- Whitecollar

```
L A T N E M N O R I V N E N B
U A T R E M O Y X G Y O T O R
D D N H B N H I R S C H I S P
G R N O I S S E C C U S A D R
G G C A I F A M U E J O W E A
E S G V L T P P G Z R P H R L
C O R P O R A T E W L J T F L
F R E C C T E N I W T S I T O
E E L J I S V H S K O M A T C
R V R O R R J Q T N L I R O E
F U N O E U O N A U A C B G T
O A O P U I T S D V S R J L I
L F Y H B C O F H J P I T P H
K E Y I L C F R D X Y L Q U W
H K F F U V A F R O S A W N I
```

Chapter 12 White-Collar and Organized Crime

CROSSWORD PUZZLE

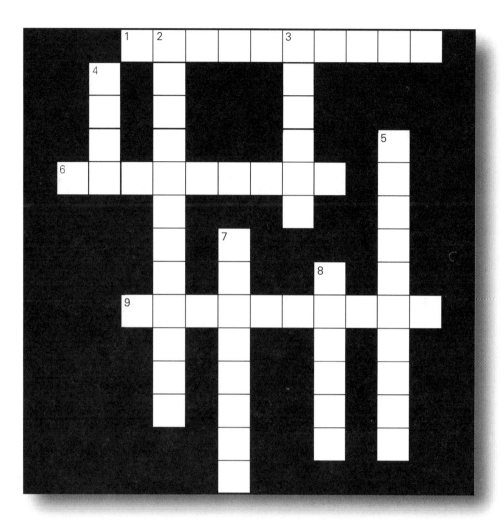

Across

1. A criminal organization of Sicilian origin.
6. A crime committed by employees acting on behalf of the company.
9. Asset _____ is the authorized seizure of items of value.

Down

2. _____ crime is a crime committed through opportunity created in the course of a legal occupation.
3. The unwritten code of organized crime which demands silence and loyalty of family members.
4. A statute intended to combat criminal conspiracies.
5. The criminologist who first defined white-collar crime.
7. The federal committee formed in 1951 to investigate organized crime.
8. _____ succession is the process by which one immigrant group succeeds another.

drug abuse and crime

CHAPTER 13

Learning Objectives

After reading this chapter, you should be able to:

1. Discuss drug-defined and drug-related crimes
2. Define dangerous drugs, and identify the characteristics of psychoactive substances
3. Describe drug trafficking and government efforts to curtail it
4. Identify the pros and cons of various drug control strategies
5. Explain arguments for and against drug legalization and decriminalization

CHAPTER SUMMARY

Drugs, and their relationship to crime, is one of the most significant policy issues today. There are a number of sources of data on drug abuse in the United States; this chapter reviews the findings of several recent surveys of both juveniles and adults. The costs of drug abuse are extremely difficult to measure, as they include not only measurable expenditures (law enforcement activities, criminal justice case processing, drug-treatment programs, etc.) but also related costs (illness and death resulting from exposure to controlled substances, drug-related crime, family fragmentation caused by illegal drug use, attitudinal change, etc.) There are seven main categories of controlled substances: stimulants, depressants, cannabis, narcotics, hallucinogens, anabolic steroids, and inhalants. In addition, there is a separate eighth category, dangerous drugs, which refers to broad categories or classes of controlled substances other than cocaine, opiates, and cannabis products.

Stimulants include amphetamines, cocaine, crack, and methamphetamine. These drugs stimulate the central nervous system. Depressants include barbiturates, sedatives, and tranquilizers and may be used both legitimately (to reduce anxiety or elevate mood) or illegitimately. Cannabis, or marijuana, is nonaddictive. Research suggests that it may be used to treat pain and glaucoma, and as a supplement to cancer chemotherapy. Most marijuana used in the United States is either grown in the country or brought in from Mexico. Narcotics such as opium, morphine, heroine, and codeine have both legitimate and illegitimate uses. Frequent users may build up tolerances to the drugs and require ever-increasing doses to obtain the desired effects. Hallucinogens have no official legitimate use. They produce hallucinations and perceptual distortions. Anabolic steroids are used legitimately for weight gain and the treatment of certain disorders, such as arthritis. They may be used illegally by body builders and professional athletes trying to build body bulk or increase strength. Inhalants are volatile substances which depress the central nervous system. They are sometimes considered gateway drugs because they may initiate young people into illicit drug use. Pharmaceutical diversion, primarily of depressants, stimulants, and anabolic steroids, occurs through illegal prescribing by physicians and illegal dispensing by pharmacists. Designer drugs are manufactured by slightly altering the chemical makeup of other illegal or controlled drugs.

Drug trafficking includes the manufacturing, distributing, dispensing, importing, and exporting of a controlled or counterfeit substance. Most cocaine comes into the United States from the Western Hemisphere, especially from South America; it is smuggled in primarily aboard maritime vessels. The Drug Enforcement Agency's (DEA) heroin signature program tracks heroin trafficking and has found that the majority of heroin in the United States originates in South America.

Drug-defined crimes include violations of laws prohibiting or regulating the possession, use, or distribution of illegal drugs. Drug-related crimes are crimes in which drugs contribute to the offense. There is clear evidence of a strong relationship between drug use and crime. The Arrestee Drug Abuse Monitoring Program attempts to measure the degree to which criminal offenders use controlled substances as a way of understanding the connection between drugs and crime. Drugs are also linked to official corruption; studies of police corruption have found that much illegal police activity was drug related. Corrections officials may also be involved in drug-related corruption.

The text discusses the history of drug-control policy in the United States, beginning with the 1906 federal Food and Drug Act, which required manufacturers to list their ingredients and specifically targeted mood-altering chemicals. The Comprehensive Drug Abuse Prevention and Control Act, passed in 1970, may be the most comprehensive piece of federal legislation to address controlled substances. The Violent Crime Control and Law Enforcement Act of 1994 also included a number of drug-related provisions. There are five main types of policy initiatives in the fight against illicit drugs. Current policy emphasizes antidrug legislation and strict enforcement. Interdiction is an international drug-control policy that focuses on stopping drugs from entering the country illegally. Crop control involves the eradication of drug crops both in the United States and abroad. Asset forfeiture allows judicial representatives to seize any items that were involved in drug trafficking or

Chapter 13 Drug Abuse and Crime

sale. Antidrug education and drug treatment have become extremely popular recently. School-based programs such as D.A.R.E. have increased, although recent research has begun to question the effectiveness of D.A.R.E.-type interventions.

The Office of National Drug Control Policy was established in 1988, with the mission of establishing policies, priorities, and objectives for the national drug-control program. The goals of the program are to reduce illicit drug use, manufacturing, and trafficking; to reduce drug-related crime and violence; and to ameliorate drug-related health consequences.

The war on drugs has been extremely expensive. As a result of the war on drugs, all phases of the criminal justice system have become drug-driven; the civil justice system has also been affected. Rates of imprisonment for drug offenders has increased significantly as a result of strict enforcement and a policy of incarceration.

Alternative drug-control policies are based on the assumption that drug abuse will never be eliminated. Decriminalization involves the reduction of criminal penalties associated with personal possession of a controlled substance. Legalization eliminates the laws and penalties that prohibit the production, sale, distribution, and possession of a controlled substance. There are a variety of arguments for and against legalization of drugs in the United States today.

KEY CONCEPTS

Arrestee Drug Abuse Monitoring (ADAM) Program a National Institute of Justice program that tracks trends in the prevalence and types of drug use among booked arrestees in urban areas.

dangerous drug A term used by the Drug Enforcement Administration to refer to "broad categories or classes of controlled substances other than cocaine, opiates, and cannabis products." Amphetamines, methamphetamines, PCP (phencyclidine), LSD, methcathinone, and "designer drugs" are all considered to be dangerous drugs.

decriminalization (of drugs) The reduction of criminal penalties associated with the personal possession of a controlled substance.

drug-defined crime A violation of the laws prohibiting or regulating the possessing, use, or distribution of illegal drugs.

drug-related crime A crime in which drugs contribute to the offense (excluding violations of drug laws).

drug trafficking Manufacturing, distributing, dispensing, importing, and exporting (or possession with intent to do the same) a controlled substance or a counterfeit substance.[1]

heroin signature program (HSP) A Drug Enforcement Administration program that identifies the geographic source of a heroin sample through the detection of specific chemical characteristics in the sample peculiar to the source area.

interdiction An international drug control policy that aims to stop drugs from entering the country illegally.

legalization (of drugs) Elimination of the laws and associated criminal penalties that prohibit the production, sale, distribution, and possession of a controlled substance.

National Household Survey on Drug Abuse (NHSDA) A national survey of illicit drug use among people 12 years of age and older that is conducted annually by the Substance Abuse and Mental Health Services Administration.

---

1 Bureau of Justice Statistics, Drugs, *Crime and the Justice System* (Washington, D.C.: U.S. Department of Justice, December 1992), p. 181.

Office of National Drug Control Policy (ONDCP) A national office charged by Congress with establishing policies, priorities, and objectives for the nation's drug-control program. ONDCP is responsible for developing and disseminating the *National Drug-Control Strategy*.

pharmaceutical diversion The process by which legitimately manufactured controlled substances are diverted for illicit use.

psychoactive substance A substance that affects the mind, mental processes, or emotions.

CHAPTER OUTLINE

I. Introduction _____

II. History of Drug Abuse in the United States _____

    A. Extent of Abuse _____

    B. Young People and Drugs _____

    C. Costs of Abuse _____

III. Types of Illegal Drugs _____

    A. Stimulants _____

    B. Depressants _____

    C. Cannabis _____

    D. Narcotics _____

    E. Hallucinogens _____

    F. Anabolic Steroids _____

    G. Inhalants _____

    H. Pharmaceutical Diversion and Designer Drugs _____

Chapter 13 Drug Abuse and Crime

    IV. Drug Trafficking _____

    V. Drugs and Crime _____

        A. Illegal Drugs and Official Corruption _____

    VI. Social Policy and Drug Abuse _____

        A. Recent Legislation _____

        B. Drug-Control Strategies _____

        C. The National Drug-Control Policy _____

        D. Policy Consequences _____

        E. Alternative Drug Policies _____

DISCUSSION QUESTIONS

These discussion questions are found in the textbook at the end of the chapter. Your instructor may want to focus on these questions at the conclusion of the lecture on Chapter 13.

1. This book emphasizes a social problems versus social responsibility theme. Which of the social policy approaches to controlling drug abuse discussed in this chapter (if any) appear to be predicated upon a social problems approach? Which (if any) are predicated upon a social responsibility approach? Explain the nature of the relationship.

2. What are some of the costs of illicit drug use in the United States today? Which costs can be more easily reduced than others? How would you reduce the cost of illegal drug use?

3. What is the difference between decriminalization and legalization? Should drug use remain illegal? What do you think of the arguments in favor of legalization? Those against?

4. What is the difference between drug-defined and drug-related crime? Which form of crime is more difficult to address? Why?

5. What is *asset forfeiture*? How has asset forfeiture been used in the fight against controlled substances? How have recent U.S. Supreme Court decisions limited federal asset seizures? Do you agree that such limitations were necessary? Why or why not?

STUDENT EXERCISES

Activity 1

Write a short paper discussing the advantages and disadvantages of legalizing marijuana in the United States. Include your personal opinion on the question of legalization and explain why you feel this way.

Activity 2

Go to the Drug Enforcement Administration Web site (http://www.usdoj.gov/dea) and answer the following questions:

1. What is the "red ribbon campaign," and how did it begin?

2. What is the DEA's Mobile Enforcement Team?

3. Explain the DEA's Demand Reduction Program, including its goals and objectives.

4. What was Operation Zorro II, and why was it unique?

5. What was the French Connection?

6. What is the mission of the DEA?

Chapter 13 Drug Abuse and Crime

7. If you are convicted of your second offense of marijuana trafficking with 100–999 plants, what would the penalty be?

CRIMINOLOGY TODAY ON THE WEB

http://www.usdoj.gov/dea
This is the home page of the Drug Enforcement Administration.

http://www.dare.com
This is the official Web site for D.A.R.E.

http://www.nida.nih.gov
This is the home page of the National Institute on Drug Abuse.

http://www.undcp.org
This is the home page of the United Nations Office for Drug Control and Crime Prevention.

http://www.rand.org/multi/dprc
This is the home page for the Drug Policy Research Center at Rand.

http://www.DrugWatch.org
This is the Web site for Drug Watch International.

http://virlib.ncjrs.org/DrugsAndCrime.asp
This Web site provides information on resources available from the National Criminal Justice Reference Service that relate to drugs and crime.

http://www.ojp.usdoj.gov/bjs/drugs.htm
This Web site provides statistics on drugs and crime from the Bureau of Justice Statistics.

http://www.samhsa.gov
This is the home page of the Substance Abuse and Mental Health Services Administration.

http://www.whitehousedrugpolicy.gov
This is the home page of the Office of National Drug Control Policy.

http://www.lindesmith.org
This is the home page of the Lindesmith Center, the leading independent drug policy institute in the United States.

http://www.mpp.org
This is the home page of the Marijuana Policy Project, a nonprofit organization in the District of Columbia with the goal of providing the marijuana law reform movement with full-time lobbying on the federal level.

http://www.sadd.org
This is the home page of Students Against Destructive Decisions, a peer leadership organization dedicated to preventing underage drinking and drug use.

PRACTICE QUESTIONS

True/False

_____ 1. During the nineteenth century, the use of illegal drugs was widespread throughout all levels of society.

_____ 2. In general, rates of illicit drug use decline with age.

_____ 3. The rate of illicit drug use is correlated with employment status.

_____ 4. The results of the *National Household Survey on Drug Abuse* are extremely accurate.

_____ 5. The *Monitoring the Future* study provides data primarily on drug abuse among adults.

_____ 6. The cost of enforcing drug laws is a direct cost of illegal drug use.

_____ 7. *Ice, crystal,* and *glass* are street names for crystallized methamphetamine.

_____ 8. Marijuana is nonaddictive.

_____ 9. Most inhalants are easily available.

_____ 10. Most cocaine entering the United States is smuggled via commercial airplanes.

_____ 11. Committing a violent crime while under the influence of an illegal drug is an example of a drug-related crime.

_____ 12. According to the ADAM program, arrestee drug use varies significantly by city.

_____ 13. Only a small percentage of illegal police activity is drug related.

_____ 14. The Narcotic Control Act required the complete removal of heroin from all medicines.

_____ 15. Interdiction is an international drug-control policy.

_____ 16. The Office of National Drug-Control Policy is responsible for producing a national drug-control strategy.

_____ 17. Decriminalization is based on the assumption that drug abuse will never be eliminated.

Fill in the Blank

18. _____ substances were widely accepted during the hippie movement of the 1960s.

19. Recently, heroin use among eighth graders has _____.

20. _____ are used illegally by people trying to produce feelings of competence and power and a state of excitability.

21. Research suggests that _____ can be used in the treatment of glaucoma.

22. LSD falls into the _____ category of drugs.

23. Major heroin and cocaine trafficking routes are sometimes called _____.

24. The most commonly used drug among adult arrestees is _____.

Chapter 13 Drug Abuse and Crime

25. Any and all drugs could be bought and sold in the United States without restriction prior to the year _____.

26. The _____ Act mandated Prohibition.

Multiple Choice

27. During the late nineteenth century, which of the following people would have been most likely to be abusing drugs (other than opium)?
    a. An upper-class merchant
    b. A servant
    c. An artist
    d. A factor worker

28. The highest rate of illicit drug use in 1999 was found among persons aged _____ years.
    a. 12–17
    b. 18–20
    c. 21–25
    d. 26–29

29. Illicit drug use is highly correlated with
    a. current employment status.
    b. educational status.
    c. both a and b
    d. neither a nor b

30. According to the *Monitoring the Future* study, which of the following statements about high school seniors (twelfth-graders) is true?
    a. Past-year use of any illicit drug declined significantly since 1997.
    b. Cocaine use decreased from 1999 to 2000.
    c. Use of hallucinogens remained stable from 1999 to 2000.
    d. There has been a decrease in the use of ecstacy from 1999 to 2000.

31. _____ is the leading cause of death of Hispanic men between the ages of 25 and 44.
    a. Drug overdose
    b. Cancer
    c. AIDS
    d. Homicide

32. The _____ category of drugs includes barbiturates, sedatives, and tranquilizers.
    a. stimulant
    b. cannabis
    c. narcotic
    d. depressant

33. _____ have no official legitimate use.
    a. Narcotics
    b. Depressants
    c. Stimulants
    d. Hallucinogens

34. _____ are produced by slightly changing the chemical makeup of illegal or controlled substances.
    a. Designer drugs
    b. Inhalants
    c. Hallucinogens
    d. Anabolic steroids

35. Most cocaine entering the United States originates in
    a. South America.
    b. Central America.
    c. Asia.
    d. Mexico.

36. Which of the following statements about the relationship between drug use and crime is true?
    a. Drug abuse causes criminal behavior to increase.
    b. Criminal behavior causes drug abuse to increase.
    c. Both drug abuse and criminal behavior are caused by a third factor.
    d. There is a clear relationship between drug abuse and crime.

37. The Pure Food and Drug Act
    a. restricted the importation and distribution of opium.
    b. required manufacturers to list their ingredients
    c. controlled the sale and possession of marijuana.
    d. outlawed the sale and distribution of medicines containing opium.

38. The goal of a "Drug-Free America by 1995" was part of the federal _____ Act
    a. Controlled Substances
    b. Anti-Drug Abuse
    c. Comprehensive Drug Abuse Prevention and Control
    d. Violent Crime Control and Law Enforcement

39. _____ strategies focus on stopping drugs from entering the United States illegally.
    a. Source control
    b. Interdiction
    c. Asset forfeiture
    d. Crop control

40. Which of the following is not an argument in favor of legalization?
    a. Legalization could lower the price of drugs.
    b. Legalization would reduce the opportunity for official corruption.
    c. Drug laws are enforceable.
    d. Legalization would result in increased tax revenues.

Chapter 13 Drug Abuse and Crime

WORD SEARCH PUZZLE

Decriminalize
Diversion
Interdiction
Legalization
Pharmaceutical
Psychoactive
Substances
Trafficking

```
P N N C N B Z H N S P G E
H C O O B L P W V U P D E
A T N I Q K M B R B C R P
R O R T S T P B Z L S M G S
M M C A T R C Z Y U T L H Y
A L J Z F N E I N K A G F C
C Z J I L F F V D Q N O H H
E Z I L A N I M I R C E D O
U E H A A B Y C K D E J R A
T U T G C J R S K I S T C C
I M X E E Z E L P I M Q N T
C A V L S G N N H I N T E I
A S N B Q Z T B C H Z G S V
L L U C A Z K L K T M R Q E
```

CROSSWORD PUZZLE

Across

1. A _____ substance affects the mind, mental processes, or emotions.
2. Reducing criminal penalties associated with the personal possession of a controlled substance.
3. Eliminating the laws that prohibit the possession and sale of controlled substances.
5. An international drug-control policy trying to stop drugs from entering the country illegally.
6. Drug _____ involves manufacturing and distributing controlled substances.
7. Asset _____ is the authorized seizure of money or other things of value.

Down

1. _____ diversion involves diverting legitimately manufactured controlled substances for illicit use.
4. _____ drugs are created by altering the chemical makeup of other illegal drugs.

technology and crime

Learning Objectives

After reading this chapter, you should be able to:

1. Describe the nature of high-technology and computer crime
2. Describe some high-technology crime countermeasures
3. Explain various computer-security techniques, including data encryption
4. Discuss the nature of a threat analysis, and explain how one might be conducted
5. Explain the nature and potential usefulness of DNA fingerprinting

CHAPTER SUMMARY

This chapter discusses the links between technology and crime. Technology, which facilitates new forms of criminal behavior, can be used both by criminals and by those who enforce the law. Because of the increasing value of information, high-tech criminals have taken a variety of routes to obtain illegitimate access to computerized information. Some criminals may focus simply on destroying or altering information rather than copying it. Technically, computer crime is defined as any violation of a federal or state computer crime statute. The text discusses several typologies of computer crime. Some authors use the term *cybercrime* to refer to crimes involving the use of computers or the manipulation of digital data. One example of cybercrime is phone phreaking, which involves the illegitimate use of dial-up access codes and other restricted technical information to avoid long-distance charges or to steal cellular telephone numbers and access codes. In addition, some computer crime is malicious rather than being committed for financial gain; this includes the creation and transmission of computer viruses, worms, and other malicious forms of programming code.

Originally, most jurisdictions in the United States attempted to prosecute unauthorized computer access under preexisting property crime statutes. However, today, all states and the federal government have developed computer crime statutes specifically applicable to invasive activities aimed at illegally accessing stored information. There are a variety of federal statutes of relevance to crimes committed with or against computer equipment and software. One of the most controversial has been the Computer Decency Act (CDA), signed into law in 1996, which focused on protecting minors from harmful material on the Internet by making it a crime to knowingly transmit obscene or indecent material to a recipient under the age of 18. However, the ACLU filed suit against the federal government, challenging the constitutionality of the CDA's provisions relating to the transmission of obscene material to minors. After a federal district court ruled that the provisions violated the First Amendment guarantees of free speech, the case was appealed to the U.S. Supreme Court, which upheld the lower court's ruling in the 1997 case of *Reno* v. *ACLU*. Individual state laws are rarely modeled after federal legislation and generally vary greatly among states. Some experts distinguish among several categories of crimes involving computers, including computer crime, computer-related crime, and computer abuse.

Many computer criminals come from the hacker subculture. Hackers and hacker identities are a product of cyberspace, which exists only within electronic networks. The text discusses a typology of hackers that is based on psychological characteristics. In addition, some high-tech crimes are committed by professional criminals who use technology to commit serious crimes, such as the theft of money. The World Wide Web may also be used to facilitate criminal activity, such as the computerized transmission of illegal pornography among pedophiles. Computer crime also shares a number of characteristics with white-collar crime.

The Internet is the world's largest computer network; its growth has encouraged hackers and computer criminals to attack it through the creation and development of programs such as viruses and worms. Because information and property can be transmitted through data networks, cybercriminals are not affected by national boundaries, nor do they have to be anywhere near the location of the victim to commit crimes. However, law enforcement agencies are still affected by geographic boundaries and may still have to deal with the difficulties of international cooperation.

Technology helps both criminals and criminal justice personnel; law enforcement capabilities and criminally useful technologies usually leapfrog each other. Key technology in law enforcement service today include traffic radar, computer databases of known offenders, machine-based expert systems, cellular communications, electronic eavesdropping, DNA analysis, and less-than-lethal weapons. DNA profiling has become an important tool for criminal justice, and all states have passed legislation requiring convicted offenders to provide samples for DNA databasing.

Computers themselves may serve as tools in the fight against crime. Technologies such as AFIS (automated fingerprint identification systems) and online criminal information services (NCIC, VICAP, etc.) facilitate the work of law enforcement agents. Expert systems that attempt to duplicate the decision-making processes used by skilled investigators may be used in offender profiling. Combating computer crime necessarily involves a realistic threat analysis that identifies organizational perils so that strategies to deal with them can be introduced. One powerful tool is the audit trail. Currently, few police departments have specialized computer crime units or personnel skilled in the investigation of computer crime, and many place a low priority on the investigation of computer crime.

Any effective policy for dealing with computer criminals must recognize various issues associated with personal freedoms and individual rights and must address the issues of deterrence. Sanctions that may be effective in deterring high-tech offenders include confiscating equipment used to commit a computer crime, limiting the offender's use of computers, and restricting the offender's freedom to accept jobs involving computers. One key policy issue is whether the First Amendment's protection of free speech applies to electronic communications. Private groups such as the Electronic Frontier Foundation (EFF) have been formed to focus on the protection of constitutional principles as new communications technologies emerge.

KEY CONCEPTS

audit trail A sequential record of computer system activities that enables auditors to reconstruct, review, and examine the sequence of states and activities surrounding each event in one or more related transactions from inception to output of final results back to inception.

Carnivore A network diagnostic tool that is capable of assisting in criminal investigations by monitoring and capturing large amount of Internet traffic. Also called *Omnivore*.

Communications Decency Act A federal statute signed into law in 1996, the CDA is Title 5 of the federal Telecommunications Act of 1996 (Public Law 104-104, 110 Stat. 56). The law sought to protect minors from harmful material on the Internet and a portion of the CDA criminalized the knowing transmission of obscene or indecent messages to any recipient under 18 years of age. In 1997, however, in the case of *Reno* v. *ACLU* (521 US 844), the U.S. Supreme Court found the bulk of the CDA to be unconstitutional, ruling that it contravenes First Amendment free speech guarantees.

Computer abuse Any incident without color of right associated with computer technology in which a victim suffered or could have suffered loss, and/or a perpetrator by intention made or could have made gain.[1]

computer crime Any violation of a federal or state computer crime statute. See also **cybercrime**.

computer-related crime Any illegal act for which knowledge of computer technology is involved for its perpetration, investigation, or prosecution.

computer virus A set of computer instructions that propagates copies or versions of itself into computer programs or data when it is executed.

cybercrime Crime committed with the use of computers or via the manipulation of digital forms of data. See also **computer crime**.

cyberspace The computer-created matrix of virtual possibilities, including online services, wherein human beings interact with one another and with the technology itself.

data encryption The process by which information is encoded, making it unreadable to all but its intended recipients.

---

[1] This and other computer crime-related terms are adapted from Donn B. Parker, *Computer Crime: Criminal Justice Resource Manual* (Washington, D.C.: National Institute of Justice, 1989).

***Daubert* standard** A test of scientific acceptability applicable to the gathering of evidence in criminal cases.

Digital Theft Deterrence and Copyright Damages Improvement Act Passed in 1999, this federal law (Public Law 106-160) attempted to combat software piracy and other forms of digital theft by amending Section 504(c) of the Copyright Act, thereby increasing the amount of damages that could potentially be awarded in cases of copyright infringement.

DNA fingerprinting The use of biological residue found at the scene of a crime for genetic comparisons in aiding the identification of criminal suspects. Also called *DNA profiling*.

expert systems Computer hardware and software that attempt to duplicate the decision-making processes used by skilled investigators in the analysis of evidence and in the recognition of patterns which such evidence might represent.

hacker A person who uses computers for exploration and exploitation.

identity theft The unauthorized use of another individual's personal identity to fraudulently obtain money, goods, or services, to avoid the payment of debt, or to avoid criminal prosecution.

Internet The world's largest computer network.

No Electronic Theft Act (NETA/NETAct) A 1997 federal law (Public Law 105-147) that criminalizes the willful infringement of copyrighted works, including by electronic means, even when the infringing party derives no direct financial benefit from the infringement (such as when pirated software is freely distributed online). In keeping with requirements of the NETA, the U.S. Sentencing Commission enacted amendments to its guidelines on April 6, 2000, to increase penalties associated with electronic theft.

phone phreak A person who uses switched, dialed-access telephone services for exploration and exploitation.

software piracy The unauthorized and illegal copying of software programs.

TEMPEST A standard developed by the U.S. government that requires that electromagnetic emanations from computers designated as "secure" be below levels that would allow radio receiving equipment to "read" the data being computed.

threat analysis A complete and thorough assessment of the kinds of perils facing an organization. Also called *risk analysis*.

CHAPTER OUTLINE

I. Introduction _____

II. Crime and Technology _____

III. High Technology and Criminal Opportunity _____

    A. Technology and Criminal Mischief _____

Chapter 14 Technology and Crime

    B. Computer Crime and the Law _____

IV. A Profile of Computer Criminals _____

    A. The History and Nature of Hacking _____

    B. Computer Crime as a Form of White-Collar Crime _____

V. The Information Superhighway and Data Security _____

VI. Technology in the Fight against Crime _____

    A. DNA Fingerprinting _____

    B. Computers as Crime-Fighting Tools _____

VII. Combating Computer Crime _____

    A. Police Investigation of Computer Crime _____

    B. Dealing with Computer Criminals _____

VIII. Policy Issues: Personal Freedoms in the Information Age _____

    A. Frontier Foundation _____

IX. What the Future Holds _____

DISCUSSION QUESTIONS

These discussion questions are found in the textbook at the end of the chapter. Your instructor may want to focus on these questions at the conclusion of the lecture on Chapter 14.

1. This book emphasizes a social problems versus social responsibility theme. Which perspective best explains the involvement of capable individuals in criminal activity necessitating high-tech skills? What is the best way to deal with such criminals?

2. What is the difference between high-tech crime and traditional forms of criminal activity? Will the high-tech crimes of today continue to be the high-tech crimes of tomorrow? Why or why not?

3. What forms of high-tech crime can you imagine which this chapter has not discussed? Describe each briefly.

4. Do you believe that high-tech crimes will eventually surpass the abilities of enforcement agents to prevent or solve them? Why or why not?

5. What different kinds of high-tech offenders can you imagine? What is the best way to deal with each type offender? Give reasons for your answers.

STUDENT EXERCISES

Activity 1

Select three theories that you have discussed in previous chapters and discuss how each of these might explain the actions of high-tech offenders.

Activity 2

Visit a local, county, or state police department in your area and find out how they handle cases of computer crime.

CRIMINOLOGY TODAY ON THE WEB

http://www.eff.org

This is the home page of the Electronic Frontier Foundation.

http://www.usdoj.gov/criminal/cybercrime/index.html

This is the home page of the U.S. Department of Justice Criminal Division's Computer Crime and Intellectual Property Section.

Chapter 14 Technology and Crime

http://www.nipc.gov

This is the home page of the National Infrastructure Protection Center.

http://www.fbi.gov/hq/lab/carnivore/carnivore.htm

This Web site provides information on the FBI's Carnivore Diagnostic Tool.

http://www.siia.net

This is the home page of the Software and Information Industry Association.

http://www.wired.com/news/lovebug

This Web site provides information on the Love Bug virus.

http://www.cnn.com/US/9703/cda.scotus

This CNN site provides information on the case of *Reno* v. *ACLU* and the history of the debate over the Communications Decency Act.

http://www.cpsr.org

This is the home page of Computer Professionals for Social Responsibility.

PRACTICE QUESTIONS

True/False

_____ 1. Most computer systems today have security procedures installed to prevent computer trespass.

_____ 2. According to David Carter, using one computer to obtain information stored in another computer is an example of a crime associated with the prevalence of computers.

_____ 3. Vietnam has extremely low rates of illegal software use.

_____ 4. The creation and transmission of computer viruses is committed for financial gain.

_____ 5. A PDA may be infected by a computer virus.

_____ 6. The person who sent the Love Bug computer virus out onto the Internet was eventually convicted of a crime.

_____ 7. The average hacker is female.

_____ 8. Phone phreaking is one of the earliest forms of hacking.

_____ 9. Money is only information.

_____ 10. Former Vice President Al Gore was a strong proponent of the information superhighway.

_____ 11. The Spiderman snare is a discolike strobe light which quickly disorients human targets.

_____ 12. DNA evidence has not yet been used to exonerate defendants sentenced to incarceration.

_____ 13. Expert systems such as NCAVC may eventually replace human investigators.

_____ 14. Most small businesses today have a clear understanding of the need for security in the use of their computers.

_____ 15. Most local police departments do not have specialized computer crime units.

_____ 16. Encryption technology was developed in the 1980s.

Fill in the Blank

17. Computer _____ involves remote access to targeted machines.

18. _____ is a form of software piracy that involves purchasing a single licensed copy of software and loading the same copy onto several computers.

19. A computer _____ is a program designed to invade a computer system and modify the way it operates or alter the information it stores.

20. The Communications Decency Act was challenged on the grounds that it contravened the _____ Amendment to the U.S. Constitution.

21. _____ see hacking itself as a game.

22. In some jurisdictions, _____ systems involve computers prompting police dispatchers for important information which allows them to distinguish locations within a city.

23. The _____ police were the first national police force in the world to begin routine collection of DNA samples from anyone involved in a serious crime.

24. The FBI's National Center for the Analysis of Violent Crime is an example of a(n) _____ system.

25. The FBI's National Computer Crime Squad investigates violations of the federal _____ Act.

26. The FBI has created a network "sniffer" known as _____.

Multiple Choice

27. The person most likely to invade a computer is
    a. a hacker.
    b. an unauthorized user.
    c. a current employee.
    d. a skilled computer amateur.

28. _____ is/are an example of the "theft" category of computer crime.
    a. Viruses
    b. Hacking
    c. Software piracy
    d. Money laundering

29. According to the Software and Information Industry Association, _____ involves selling stand-alone software that was intended to be bundled with specific accompanying hardware.
    a. softlifting
    b. software counterfeiting
    c. renting
    d. OEM unbundling

Chapter 14 Technology and Crime

30. Which of the following is not an example of a destructive computer program?
    a. A virus
    b. A logic bomb
    c. A Trojan horse
    d. The Spiderman snare

31. The _____ Act criminalized the willful infringement of copyrighted works.
    a. No Electronic Theft
    b. Communications Decency
    c. Digital Theft Deterrence and Copyright Damages
    d. National Stolen Property

32. _____ is defined as any incident without color of right associated with computer technology in which a victim suffered or could have suffered loss and/or a perpetrator intentionally made or could have made gain.
    a. Computer crime
    b. Computer-related crime
    c. Computer abuse
    d. Cybercrime

33. _____ are malicious hackers who deliberately cause damage with no apparent gain for themselves.
    a. Explorers
    b. Scamps
    c. Game players
    d. Vandals

34. The _____ was created by President Clinton in 1996.
    a. Commission on Critical Infrastructure Protection
    b. National Infrastructure Protection Center
    c. President's Working Group on Unlawful Conduct on the Internet
    d. National Cybercrime Training Partnership

35. In the case of _____, the U.S. Supreme Court held that for scientific evidence to be admissible in court, the test or procedure must generally be accepted by the relevant scientific community.
    a. *Frye* v. *United States*
    b. *Reno* v. *ACLU*
    c. *Daubert* v. *Merrell Dow Pharmaceuticals, Inc.*
    d. none of the above

36. Bulletproof software, which compares a bullet's ballistic characteristics with those stored in a database, was developed by
    a. the FBI.
    b. the Police Executive Research Forum.
    c. the Bureau of Alcohol, Tobacco, and Firearms.
    d. the Bureau of Justice Statistics.

37. A(n) _____ records the activities of computer operators surrounding each event in a transaction.
    a. threat analysis
    b. audit trail
    c. DNA profile
    d. expert systems analysis

38. Carnivore is being challenged on the grounds of
    a. freedom of speech.
    b. First Amendment issues.
    c. the right to privacy.
    d. all of the above

39. Attempts to define computer crimes often result in concerns about the _____ Amendment to the Constitution.
    a. First
    b. Fifth
    c. Sixth
    d. Eighth

40. Key escrow encryption is also known as
    a. clipper.
    b. threat analysis.
    c. TEMPEST.
    d. Carnivore.

Chapter 14 Technology and Crime

WORD SEARCH PUZZLE

Audit
Carnivore
Cybercrime
Cyberspace
Daubert
Hacker

Internet
Piracy
Software
TEMPEST
Threat
Virus

```
C W G T R R V T Q A R J B
Y R Y A R A R S T I M Q V
B M J H U E K J W H E A N
E N H D B R T G Q Z Y H E
R C I U K O W U J U A L T
C T A Q S V T K C C H S Q
R D H P I I E I K W E Q E
I K S R S N N E A P R Y N
M A U Z E R R Z M R O R E
E S D W J A E E Z H G O P
I B Y F W C T B T M O T I
I Q K T Z V N H Y K X M H
E P F J Z P I R A C Y J Q
Z O I P P L N Y U R L J M
S O T I J Y W V O E F A I
```

CROSSWORD PUZZLE

Across

2. The computer-created matrix of virtual possibilities.
7. The world's largest computer network.
8. A set of computer instructions that propagates copies of itself into computer programs.
10. A person who uses computers for exploration and exploitation.

Down

1. The _____ standard is a test of scientific acceptability of evidence gathering in criminal cases.
2. Crime committed with the use of computers or the manipulation of digital forms of data.
3. Data _____ is the process by which information is encoded.
4. A phone _____ uses telephone services for exploration and exploitation.
5. A network diagnostic tool that can assist in criminal investigations by capturing Internet traffic.
6. A government standard for electromagnetic emanations from secure computers.
9. _____ analysis is a thorough assessment of the kinds of perils facing an organization.

criminology and social policy

Chapter 15

Learning Objectives

After reading this chapter, you should be able to:

1. Distinguish between the social problems approach and the social responsibility approach to crime control
2. Recognize and understand the different types of crime control strategies
3. Relate various crime control strategies to recent American crime control policy initiatives
4. Describe the history and the current state of the victims' movement in this country

CHAPTER SUMMARY

Today's public policymakers are faced with a variety of crime-related problems and issues. Public or social policy is a course of action that government takes in an effort to solve a problem or achieve an end. In many cases it appears that crime-fighting policies may be more the result of politics than they are the direct outcome of social science research and data.

Federal involvement in crime began during the Hoover administration, when Hoover established the National Commission on Law Observance and Enforcement (the Wickersham Commission). Hoover's administration developed a wide variety of policy initiatives in the areas of police, courts, and corrections, using experts in a number of criminal justice–related fields; many of his reforms were effective. One key problem with policymaking groups such as the Wickersham Commission was that they failed to include broad representation of racial or ethnic minorities.

After World War II, the United States experienced a period of economic prosperity and lowered crime rates that lasted until the 1960s. During the Kennedy administration, crime and crime control were important political issues. Crime and violence issues were again emphasized during the Johnson administration. Johnson established the President's Commission on Law Enforcement and Administration of Justice, which reported that crime was the inevitable result of poverty, unemployment, low education levels, and other social an economic disadvantages. One result of the Commission's report was passage of the Omnibus Crime Bill and Safe Streets Act of 1967. Title I of this act created the Law Enforcement Assistance Administration (LEAA), which provided technical and financial assistance to states for the purpose of improving and strengthening law enforcement activities at the local level. President Nixon developed the concept of a "war on crime," emphasizing tough-on-crime policies and reducing interest in the rights of the accused. Nixon commissioned the National Advisory Commission on Criminal Justice Standards and Goals, which called for improved police–community relations and enhanced communications between agencies in the criminal justice system.

President Reagan felt that the choice of a career in crime was not the result of social problems such as poverty or an unhappy childhood but was a conscious and willful choice. He emphasized holding individual offenders responsible for their crimes while reducing the focus on the root causes of crime. In support of this, Congress passed the Comprehensive Crime Control Act of 1984, which included a variety of "get tough" provisions. Reagan also developed the "war on drugs," emphasizing his belief that drugs contributed both directly and indirectly to much of the country's crime problem. He created a new cabinet-level position to coordinate federal drug-fighting efforts. During President George Bush's administration (1989–1993), the war on drugs continued to be funded by federal and state tax dollar.

During his administration, President Clinton was able to influence the development of a number of crime control initiatives already under way. He emphasized gun-control legislation, such as the Brady Handgun Violence Prevention Act. The centerpiece of the Clinton administration crime control legislation was the Violent Crime Control and Law Enforcement Act. It provided massive funding for increased law enforcement and correctional resources, increased control over firearms, expanded the federal death penalty, created drug-free zones, included federal three-strikes provisions, and increased or enhanced penalties for over 70 criminal penalties. It also had several provisions in the areas of victims' rights. Other components of the act include the Violence Against Women Act.

President George W. Bush has committed himself to some identifiable positions. He has stated that he supports executions as a deterrent, supports the death penalty for criminals as young as 17, supports mandatory sentences for repeat offenders, supports two-strikes legislation and registration for sex offenders, advocates victim notification laws, favors antistalking laws, and favors giving judges and juries more discretion in sentencing criminals. He repeatedly spoke out in favor of the death penalty while serving as governor of Texas.

Currently, there is a two-pronged approach to crime control in the United States: the social responsibility perspective and the social problems perspective. There are three main crime control strategies. Protection/avoidance strategies involve attempts to reduce criminal opportunities in some way; deterrence strategies attempt to reduce the motivation for crime by increasing the perceived certainty, severity, or swiftness of penalties; and nurturant strategies focus on preventing the development of criminality. Although many criminologists feel that a comprehensive crime control strategy would be a balanced mix of all three strategies, politicians and policymakers focus primarily on protection/avoidance and deterrence strategies and generally ignore nurturant strategies. Although many criminologists feel that criminological research is not directly influencing policy and practice, there is evidence that the conceptual use of ideas developed through criminological research has affected policymakers in a broad way.

Victims were a forgotten element of the criminal justice system until the 1960s, when renewed interest in victim issues led to the development of victim compensation laws in all states. Victim–witness assistance programs are designed to provide comfort and assistance to victims of crime and help prevent or alleviate postcrime victimization. Many states now provide for the use of victim impact statements in court; these statements are written documents describing the losses, suffering, and trauma experienced by victims or their survivors. Some states also allow victims to attend and participate in sentencing and parole hearings, and some also allow victims to testify directly at sentencing. Victim restitution involves payment of compensation to the victim by the offender and emphasizes the concept that offenders should be responsible for at least a portion of the financial obligations needed to make the victim whole again.

Currently, many criminologists expect to work closely with politicians and policymakers to develop crime control agendas based on scientific knowledge and criminological theorizing. Many critics feel that the only way to address the issues underlying high crime rates is to implement drastic policy-level changes such as drug legalization, the elimination of guns throughout the country, nightly curfews, and close control of media violence. These reforms may be unlikely because of cultural taboos rooted in citizens' demands for individual freedoms. Because of this, many feel that there may not be a solution to the crime problem. Some even suggest that crime control policies are largely symbolic and that crime will always be a part of our society.

KEY CONCEPTS

Anti-Drug Abuse Act A federal law (Public Law 99-570) enacted in 1986 that established new federal mandatory minimum sentences for drug offenses.

Brady Handgun Violence Prevention Act A federal law (Public Law 103-159) enacted in 1993 and which initiated a national background checking system for all potential gun purchasers.

Comprehensive Crime Control Act A far-reaching federal law enacted in 1984 that mandated new federal sentencing guidelines, eliminated parole at the federal level, limited the use of the insanity defense in federal criminal courts, and increased federal penalties associated with drug dealing.

deterrence strategy A crime control strategy that attempts "to diminish motivation for crime by increasing the perceived certainty, severity, or celerity of penalties."[1]

habitual offender statute A law intended to keep repeat criminal offenders behind bars. These laws sometimes come under the "three strikes and you're out" rubric.

Hate Crimes Sentencing Enhancement Act A federal law (28 U.S.C 994) enacted in 1994 as part of the *Violent Crime Control and Law Enforcement Act*, that required the U.S. Sentencing Commission to increase the penalties for crimes in which the victim was selected "because of [their] actual or perceived race, color, religion, national origin, ethnicity, gender, disability, or sexual orientation."

---

1 Bryan Vila, "A General Paradigm for Understanding Criminal Behavior: Extending Evolutionary Ecological Theory," *Criminology*, Vol. 32, No. 3 (August 1994), pp. 311-359.

Kriminalpolitik The political handling of crime. Also, a criminology-based social policy.

Law Enforcement Assistance Administration (LEAA) A federal program, established under Title 1 of the Omnibus Crime Control and Safe Streets Act of 1967, designed to provide assistance to police agencies.

National Advisory Commission on Criminal Justice Standards and Goals A federal body commissioned in 1971 by President Richard Nixon to examine the nation's criminal justice system and to set standards and goals to direct the development of the nation's criminal justice agencies.

nurturant strategy A crime control strategy that attempts "to forestall development of criminality by improving early life experiences and channeling child and adolescent development" in desirable directions. [2]

Omnibus Anti-Drug Abuse Act A federal law (Public Law 100-690) enacted in 1988 which increased federal penalties for recreational drug users and created a new cabinet-level position (known unofficially as the Drug Czar) to coordinate the drug-fighting efforts of the federal government.

Omnibus Crime Control and Safe Streets Act A federal law enacted in 1967 to eliminate the social conditions that create crime and which funded many anticrime initiatives nationwide.

postcrime victimization Problems which tend to follow from initial victimization. Also called secondary victimization.

protection/avoidance strategy crime control strategy that attempts to reduce criminal opportunities by changing people's routine activities, by increasing guardianship, or by incapacitating convicted offenders.[3]

public policy A course of action that government takes in an effort to solve a problem or to achieve an end.

restitution A criminal sanction, in particular the payment of compensation by the offender to the victim.

social epidemiology The study of social epidemics and diseases of the social order.

three-strikes provision A provision of some criminal statutes which mandates life imprisonment for criminals convicted of three violent felonies or serious drug offenses.

victim-impact statement A written document which describes the losses, suffering, and trauma experienced by the crime victim or by the victim's survivors. In jurisdictions where victim-impact statements are used, judges are expected to consider them in arriving at an appropriate sentence for the offender.

Victims of Crime Act (VOCA) A federal law enacted in 1984 that established the federal Crime Victims Fund. The fund uses monies from fines and forfeitures collected from federal offenders to supplement state support of local victims' assistance programs and state victim compensation programs.

victim-witness assistance program A program that counsels victims, orients them to the justice process, and provides a variety of other services, such as transportation to court, child care during court appearances, and referrals to social service agencies.

---

2 Vila, "A General Paradigm for Understanding Criminal Behavior."
3 Bryan Vila, "Human Nature and Crime Control: Improving the Feasibility of Nurturant Strategies," *Politics and the Life Sciences* (March 1997), pp. 3-21.

Chapter 15 Criminology and Social Policy

Violence against Women Act (VAWA) A federal law enacted as a component of the 1994 Violent Crime Control and Law Enforcement Act and which was intended to address concerns about violence against women. The law focused on improving the interstate enforcement of protection orders, providing effective training for court personnel involved with women's issues, improving the training and collaboration of police and prosecutors with victim service providers, strengthening law enforcement efforts to reduce violence against women, and on efforts to increase services to victims of violence. President Clinton signed the reauthorization of this legislation, known as the Violence against Women Act 2000, into law on October 28, 2000.

Violent Crime Control and Law Enforcement Act A federal law (Public Law 103-322) enacted in 1994 that authorized spending billions of dollars on crime prevention, law enforcement, and prison construction. It also outlawed the sale of certain types of assault weapons and enhanced federal death penalty provisions.

Wickersham Commission Created by President Herbert Hoover in 1931, and officially known as the Commission on Law Observance and Enforcement, the mandate of this commission was to develop objectives to improve justice system practices and to reinstate law's role in civilized governance. The Commission made recommendations concerning the nation's police forces, and described how to improve policing throughout America.

CHAPTER OUTLINE

I. Introduction _____

II. Federal Anticrime Initiatives _____

    A. The Hoover Administration _____

    B. Federal Policy Following World War II _____

    C. The Reagan and Bush Years _____

    D. Clinton Administration Initiatives _____

    E. The Administration of George W. Bush _____

III. Crime Control Philosophies Today _____

    A. Types of Crime Control Strategies _____

    B. International Policies _____

IV. Criminology and Social Policy _____
_____

V. The Victims' Movement _____
_____

   A. A History of the Victim _____
_____

   B. Current Directions in Victims' Rights _____
_____

   C. Victim-Impact Statements _____
_____

   D. Victim Restitution _____
_____

VI. Can We Solve the Problem of Crime? _____
_____

   A. Symbolism and Public Policy _____
_____

DISCUSSION QUESTIONS

These discussion questions are found in the textbook at the end of the chapter. Your instructor may want to focus on these questions at the conclusion of the lecture on Chapter 15.

1. This book emphasizes a social problems versus social responsibility theme. What types of anticrime social policies might be based on the social responsibility perspective? The social problems approach? Explain.

2. What are the major differences between the social problems and the social responsibility approaches? With which do you most closely identify? Why?

3. What are the three types of crime control strategies described in this chapter? Which comes closest to your own philosophy? Why?

4. Explain the social epidemiologic approach to reducing crime. In your opinion, is the approach worthwhile? Why or why not?

Chapter 15 Criminology and Social Policy

5. If you were in charge of government crime reduction efforts, what steps would you take to control crime in the United States? Why would you choose those particular approaches?

STUDENT EXERCISES

Activity 1

Your instructor will assign you a state. Obtain information on victim compensation in this state, including:

1. What are the eligibility requirements?

2. What crimes are and are not covered by the state's victim compensation program?

3. What expenses are eligible for compensation, and what compensation benefits may be awarded?

4. What other sources are available to victims?

5. How does a victim go about applying for compensation?

6. Is there a right to appeal if compensation is denied? If yes, how does this process work?

Activity 2

Review the provisions of the Violent Crime Control and Law Enforcement Act of 1994. Identify three provisions that you would consider to be protection/avoidance strategies, three provisions that you would consider to be deterrence strategies, and three provisions that you would consider to be nurturant strategies. Explain your classifications.

CRIMINOLOGY TODAY ON THE WEB

http://www4.law.cornell.edu/uscode/42/ch112.html

This site makes available Title 42, Chapter 112 of the U.S. Code, discussing federal victim compensation and victim assistance.

http://virlib.ncjrs.org/VictimsOfCrime.asp

At this Web site publications on victims of crime that are available online from the National Criminal Justice Reference Service are listed.

http://www.musc.edu/cvc

This is the home page of the National Crime Victims Research and Treatment Center, an organization studying the impact of criminal victimization on adults, children, and their families.

http://www.try-nova.org

This is the home page of the National Organization of Victims' Assistance, a private non-profit organization promoting rights and services for crime victims.

http://www.ojp.usdoj.gov/ovc

This is the home page of the Office for Victims of Crime, which was established by the 1984 Victims of Crime Act.

http://www.usinfo.state.gov/usa/infousa/laws/majorlaw/h3355_en.htm

This site makes available the text of the Violent Crime Control and Law Enforcement Act of 1994.

http://www.silicon-valley.com/3strikes.html

This Web site provides information on the California three-strikes law.

http://www.ncjrs.org/pdffiles/165369.pdf

This Web site is a link to a National Institute of Justice Research in Brief publication entitled "Three Strikes and You're Out: A Review of State Legislation," a pdf file available from the National Criminal Justice Reference Service.

http://www.crimepolicy.org

This is the home page of the Campaign for an Effective Crime Policy.

http://www.cjpf.org

This is the home page of the Criminal Justice Policy Foundation, a private nonprofit educational organization that provides information to the public about issues in federal and state anticrime proposals and promotes solutions to problems facing the criminal justice system.

PRACTICE QUESTIONS

True/False

_____ 1. The mandate of the Wickersham Commission was to explore the extent to which Prohibition was the basis for general disrespect of the law.

_____ 2. National economic expansion occurred immediately prior to World War II.

_____ 3. The crime rate in the late 1960s was less than one-third of what it is today.

_____ 4. The war on drugs was developed by President Reagan.

_____ 5. The Youth Handgun Safety Act bans the possession of handguns by juveniles under the age of 21.

Chapter 15   Criminology and Social Policy

    6. The Brady Law currently requires a five-day waiting period for the purchase of a handgun.

    7. Most crimes committed with handguns are not fatal.

    8. Drug courts were not funded by the Violent Crime Control and Law Enforcement Act.

    9. President George W. Bush is a strong supporter of capital punishment.

    10. President George W. Bush opposes abortion.

    11. Increased infant and maternal health care is an example of a deterrence strategy.

    12. Members of the American Society of Criminology feel that the organization has been extremely successful in bringing about significant changes in government policies.

    13. Victim compensation programs are generally well funded.

    14. Victim-impact statements are used prior to the sentencing of convicted criminal defendants.

    15. Restitution is applied only to adult offenders.

Fill in the Blank

16. The administration of President _____ marks the origins of federal crime control policies.

17. The concept of the war on crime was first developed by President _____.

18. The _____ Act established a national instant criminal background check system that firearms dealers contact prior to the transfer of any firearm.

19. Critics of the Violent Crime Control and Law Enforcement Act claim that it was really a _____ agenda in disguise.

20. According to research by Bryan Vila, _____ crime control strategies are more effective than others in the long run.

21. The policy approach to crime control that sees criminals as victims of social pathology is known as the social _____ perspective.

22. Improving programs to reduce the number of unwanted pregnancies is an example of the _____ strategy of crime control.

23. According to Joan Petersilia, criminologists who complain that their work is not being used by policymakers generally have an _____ model in mind.

24. The _____ theory says that victim compensation is in vogue with the voting public.

25. According to Friedman, reforms that will substantially lower the crime rate are unlikely because of _____.

Multiple Choice

26. Crime-fighting policies are probably more the result of
    a. politics.
    b. criminological research.
    c. social science data.
    d. immediate opportunities.

27. The expansion of federal crime control policies to address juvenile crime occurred during the _____ administration.
    a. Hoover
    b. Kennedy
    c. Johnson
    d. Nixon

28. Which of the following does not characterize the attitude toward federal crime control efforts during President Nixon's administration?
    a. Mandatory minimum sentences
    b. Concern for the rights of the accused
    c. Harsh penalties
    d. Reduction or abolition of parole

29. The Comprehensive Crime Control Act was signed into law by President
    a. Nixon.
    b. Carter
    c. Reagan.
    d. Bush.

30. The Hate Crimes Sentencing Enhancement Act became law during the _____ administration.
    a. Clinton
    b. Bush
    c. Reagan
    d. Kennedy

31. Under the Brady Law, purchases of handguns may be disapproved for all but which of the following reasons?
    a. The potential buyer is an illegal alien.
    b. The potential buyer has been committed to a mental institution.
    c. The potential buyer was a citizen of the United States but has renounced citizenship.
    d. The potential buyer is in the process of applying for U.S. citizenship.

32. Banning hollow-point ammunition is an example of the gun control intervention strategy of
    a. reducing the number of guns.
    b. reducing the destructiveness of guns.
    c. changing gun allocation.
    d. altering the uses or storage of guns.

33. The _____ Act provides college scholarships for students who agree to serve as police officers.
    a. Violent Crime Control and Law Enforcement
    b. Violence Against Women
    c. Victims of Crime
    d. Comprehensive Crime Control

34. Which of the following statements would you expect from President George W. Bush?
    a. The death penalty should not be used on criminals below the age of 18
    b. Life imprisonment may have a greater deterrent effect than capital punishment
    c. The parole system needs to be improved and strengthened
    d. Judges and juries should have more discretion in sentencing criminals

Chapter 15 Criminology and Social Policy

35. Protection/avoidance strategies attempt to
    a. block opportunities for crime.
    b. change the outcome of decision making that precedes a crime.
    c. change the strategic style with which people approach aspects of their lives.
    d. improve early life experiences.

36. _____ strategies include infant and maternal health care programs.
    a. Nurturant
    b. Protection/avoidance
    c. Deterrence
    d. Social epidemiology

37. Currently, political constituencies focus least on the _____ strategy of crime control.
    a. nurturant
    b. protection/avoidance
    c. deterrence
    d. social epidemiology

38. The first modern victim compensation statute was adopted by
    a. Great Britain.
    b. the United States of America.
    c. New Zealand.
    d. China.

39. _____ theory holds that compensation programs will encourage more citizens to report crime and result in more effective law enforcement programs.
    a. Humanitarian
    b. Crime prevention
    c. Government negligence
    d. Strict liability

40. The offender is directly involved in victim _____ programs.
    a. compensation
    b. restitution
    c. impact
    d. assistance

WORD SEARCH PUZZLE

Avoidance
Brady
Deterrence
Epidemiology
LEAA
Nurturant

Protection
Restitution
VOCA
Victimization
Wickersham

```
N E N E M H J L L K J Q E B
K O V M H S O F P B I Q C N
Q B I R A L R B N Q B N N H
G R G T A H E L R N Y L E T
T A R M A F S E P U Q F R N
Y D C N E Z T R A H G P R A
B Y G O L O I M E D I P E R
L L Q E V T T M L K U A T U
X A P H O U U K I Y C A E T
V I B J B S T D S T J I D R
C G D A V O I D A N C E W U
X U J G P R O T E C T I O N
V R D L M Y N T Y X N X V Q
```

Chapter 15 Criminology and Social Policy

CROSSWORD PUZZLE

Across

1. Crime control strategies that increase the perceived certainty, severity, or swiftness of penalties.
4. Social _____ is the study of diseases of the social order.
7. The _____ commission was created by President Herbert Hoover.
8. A victim _____ statement describes the victim's losses and suffering as a result of the crime.
9. _____ victimization includes problems following from the initial victimization.

Down

2. _____ laws mandate life imprisonment for criminals convicted of three violent felonies.
3. The payment of compensation by the offender to the victim.
5. Crime control strategies preventing entry into criminality by improving early life experiences.
6. The _____ law initiated a national background checking system for all potential gun purchasers.

future directions

CHAPTER 16

Learning Objectives

After reading this chapter, you should be able to:

1. Discuss future crimes and future studies
2. Identify some techniques for assessing the future
3. Describe the role of the criminological futurist in social policy development
4. Recognize the significance of an integrated theory of crime causation
5. Describe the advantages of a comparative approach to the study of crime and criminals

CHAPTER SUMMARY

People who study the future are known as futurists. Future criminology is the study of likely futures as they relate to crime and its control. There are many groups who study the future; organizations such as the Society of Police Futurists International specifically focus on future crime control policy. Globalization, the increasingly international character of social life, is affecting crime and making it impossible for U.S. policymakers to ignore crime in other countries, especially crime committed by transnational criminal organizations. Transnational crime, which involves unlawful activity undertaken and supported by organized criminal groups operating across national boundaries, is becoming a key challenge to policymakers. The globalization of crime has led to increased interest in comparative criminology or the cross-national study of crime.

Futures research is a multidisciplinary branch of operations research that attempts to facilitate long-range planning based on four elements: forecasting from the past supported by mathematical models, cross-disciplinary treatment of its subject matter, systematic use of expert judgment, and a systems-analytical approach to its problems. Futures research requires a futurist perspective. There are seven main techniques of futures research: trend extrapolation, cross-impact analysis, the Delphi method, simulations and models, environmental scanning, scenario writing, and strategic assessment. They all provide an appreciation of the risks and opportunities facing those planning for the future. Regardless of the technique, the results are no better than the data used.

Most futurists suggest that although traditional crimes (murder, rape, robbery, etc.) will continue to occur in the future, other new and emergent forms of criminality will increase in number and frequency. New types of criminality predicted by futurists include computer-based and economic crime, identity manipulation, and the increasing involvement of organized crime in toxic and nuclear waste disposal. Georgette Bennett, who helped establish the study of criminal futures as a purposeful endeavor, has predicted a number of areas of coming change, including a decline in street crime and an increase in white-collar and high-technology crimes; increasing involvement of females and the elderly in crime; and safer cities, with an increase in criminal activity in small towns and rural areas.

In addition to futures research, new and emerging criminological theories help suggest what criminology will be like in the future. During the 1980s and 1990s, a number of new and dynamic theories were developed, such as postmodernism, feminist criminology, and peacemaking criminology. One new perspective is David Farrington's risk factor prevention paradigm. This paradigm, which emphasizes identifying the key risk factors for offending and implementing prevention methods designed to counteract them, became increasingly influential in criminology during the 1990s.

The 1980s saw an emphasis on theory integration, with the ultimate goal of developing a unified theory of crime causation and prevention. Some theorists have developed theories about theories (meta-theories) which may help merge existing theories. However, there seems to be a consensus that there are too many problems for successful theory integration to occur. An alternative strategy may be a multiple-theory approach, which involves integrating only a few theories at a time.

For policymakers to be able to plan for the future, they need as much information as possible about possible eventualities. George Cole identified a number of significant changes, or "drivers," which are likely to occur in the near future and to affect crime and justice. The increasingly multicultural and heterogeneous nature of the United States will also affect crime, as it will increase anomie. Diverse heterogeneous societies such as the United States experience constant internal conflict. Disagreement about the law and social norms is common, and offenders tend to deny responsibility and to attempt to avoid capture and conviction. The chapter closes with a list of seven issues that Richter Moore, Jr. suggests are likely to concern crime control planners in the near future.

Chapter 16 Future Directions

KEY CONCEPTS

comparative criminologist A criminologist involved in the cross-national study of crime.

comparative criminology The cross-national study of crime.

cross-impact analysis A technique of futures research that attempts to analyze one trend or event in light of the occurrence or nonoccurrence of a series of related events.

Delphi Method A technique of futures research that uses repetitive questioning of experts to refine predictions.

environmental scanning "A systematic effort to identify in an elemental way future developments (trends or events) that could plausibly occur over the time horizon of interest"[1] and that might affect one's area of concern.

future criminology The study of likely futures as they impinge on crime and its control.

futures research "A multidisciplinary branch of operations research" whose principal aim "is to facilitate long-range planning based on (1) forecasting from the past supported by mathematical models, (2) cross-disciplinary treatment of its subject matter, (3) systematic use of expert judgment, and (4) a systems-analytical approach to its problems."[2]

futurist One who studies the future.

metatheory A theory about theories and the theorizing process.

scenario writing A technique, intended to predict future outcomes, which builds upon environmental scanning by attempting to assess the likelihood of a variety of possible outcomes once important trends have been identified.

strategic assessment A technique that assesses the risks and opportunities facing those who plan for the future.

trend extrapolation A technique of futures research that makes future predictions based on the projection of existing trends.

CHAPTER OUTLINE

I. Introduction _____

_____

A. Globalization _____

_____

B. Techniques of Futures Research _____

_____

II. Future Crimes _____

_____

III. The New Criminologies _____

_____

---

1 George F. Cole, "Criminal Justice in the Twenty-first Century: The Role of Futures Research," in John Klofas and Stan Stojkovic, eds., *Crime and Justice in the Year 2010* (Belmont, CA: Wadsworth, 1995).
2 Society of Police Futurists International, *PFI: The Future of Policing* (brochure), no date.

A. Theory Integration _____
_____

IV. Policies of the Future _____
_____

DISCUSSION QUESTIONS

These discussion questions are found in the textbook at the end of the chapter. Your instructor may want to focus on these questions at the conclusion of the lecture on Chapter 16.

1. This book emphasizes a social problems versus social responsibility theme. Which perspective do you think will be dominant in twenty-first century crime control planning? Why?

2. Do you believe that it is possible to know the future? What techniques are identified in this chapter for assessing possible futures? Which of these do you think holds the most promise? Why?

3. What is meant by "theory integration"? How might theory integration be achieved in the field of criminology?

4. What is comparative criminology? What are the advantages of a comparative perspective? Are there any disadvantages? If so, what are they?

STUDENT EXERCISES

Activity 1

Your instructor will divide the class into groups. The text outlines several crime-related issues which may be key issues for policymakers over the next ten years. Each group is to identify three other issues they believe may be of concern. The groups are to compare and contrast the items on their lists. Focus on the wide range of issues present among a fairly homogeneous group.

Activity 2

Your instructor will divide the class into groups. Using at least three of the theories you have studied, create an integrated theoretical model of crime causation. Outline the assumptions on which your model is based.

Chapter 16 Future Directions

CRIMINOLOGY TODAY ON THE WEB

http://www.wfs.org
This is the home page of the World Future Society.

http://www.policefuturists.org
This is the home page of the Society of Police Futurists International.

http://www.foresight.gov.uk/default1024ns.htm
This is the home page of the UK's government-led Foresight program.

http://www.futures.hawaii.edu
This is the home page of the Hawaii Research Center for Futures Studies.

http://www.ryerson.ca/~mjoppe/research/DelphiMethod.htm
This Web site provides a brief explanation of the Delphi method, including an interactive flowchart.

http://hops.wharton.upenn.edu/forecast
This is the Wharton School's Forecasting Principles Web site.

PRACTICE QUESTIONS

True/False

_____ 1. Members of the Society of Police Futurists International apply the principles of futures research to understand the world as it is likely to be in the future.

_____ 2. According to Foresight's Crime Prevention Panel, local crimes will be replaced by crimes with a global scope.

_____ 3. Most American criminal justice policies originate from issues or problems that occur outside U.S. borders.

_____ 4. Environmental scanning provides an appreciation of the risks and opportunities facing those who plan for the future.

_____ 5. Scenario writers focus on predicting a specific future.

_____ 6. According to futurist Georgette Bennett, women will become less involved in crime.

_____ 7. According to futurist L. Edward Wells, future explanations of crime will more greatly emphasize biological factors.

_____ 8. According to George F. Cole, the war on drugs will escalate in the next ten years.

_____ 9. Heterogeneous societies suffer from constant internal conflict.

Fill in the Blank

10. According to Foresight's Crime Prevention Panel, technology is leading to the growth of a(n) _____ society.

11. Comparative criminologists study crime on a(n) _____ level.

12. _____ makes future predictions based on the projection of existing trends.

13. _____ is a technique of futures research that builds upon environmental scanning.

14. A theory about theories and the theorizing process is known as a(n) _____.

15. According to Gene Stephens, multiculturalism and heterogeneity increase _____.

Multiple Choice

16. Well-known futurist _____ is the author of Future Shock.
    a. Alvin Toffler
    b. John Naisbitt
    c. Peter Drucker
    d. William Tafoya

17. The globalization of crime has led to a resurgence of interest in _____ criminology.
    a. strategic
    b. comparative interdisciplinary
    c. critical

18. Which of the following is not one of the main techniques of futures research?
    a. The Delphi method
    b. Scenario writing
    c. Cross-cultural surveys
    d. Trend extrapolation

19. The technique of futures research that involves a targeted effort to collect as much information as possible in a systematic effort to identify in an elemental way future developments that could plausibly occur over the time horizon of interest is
    a. the Delphi method.
    b. trend extrapolation.
    c. environmental scanning.
    d. scenario writing.

20. According to futurist L. Edward Wells, future explanations of crime will be more
    a. eclectic.
    b. comparative.
    c. applied.
    d. all of the above

21. Theories concerned with analyzing crime at the individual level are known as
    a. cross-national theories.
    b. microlevel theories.
    c. meta-theories.
    d. macrolevel theories.

22. Which of the following is not typically the norm in a homogeneous society?
    a. A tradition of discipline
    b. A belief in the laws
    c. An acceptance of personal responsibility
    d. Cultural diversity

Chapter 16 Future Directions

WORD SEARCH PUZZLE

Bennett
Comparative
Delphi
Extrapolation
Futurist
Levin
Metatheory

Scenario
Stephens
Strategic
Tafoya
Transnational
Trend

```
E Z M E T A T H E O R Y W M
X O I S R V Q S V A W G E L
T R A N S N A T I O N A L K
R L U A F C Z T T R S T E Q
A G I H P L E D A T U W U B
P V H P D X C N R F F T P M
O Y A S A N X A A V O E U A
L B E N N E T T P R H Y U F
A E E S X E R N M X I B A A
T E V C G E H R O C X O M C
I R K I N G B P C X S D I C
O S C D N I O H E A Z R P V
N T N C J D W K L T X P Z W
Y C M N J T J D N L S N Y L
```

CROSSWORD PUZZLE

Across

3. _____ criminology is the study of likely futures as the impinge on crime and its control.
5. Trend _____ makes predictions based on projections of existing trends.
6. _____ criminology is the cross-national study of crime.
7. _____ assessment assesses the risks and opportunities facing those planning for the future.

Down

1. _____ scanning identifies future developments that could occur over a time period of interest.
2. A theory about theories and the theorizing process.
3. One who studies the future.
4. The _____ method uses repetitive questioning of experts to refine predictions.

answers to odd numbered questions

Chapter 1
1. True
3. False
5. False
7. True
9. False
11. False
13. illegal
15. deviance
17. Paul Topinard
19. copycat violence
21. social phenomenon
23. b
25. c
27. b
29. c
31. c
33. b
35. a
37. b

Chapter 2
1. False
3. False
5. True
7. False
9. True
11. True
13. True
15. False
17. demographics
19. one-half
21. criminal homicide
23. Crime Awareness and Campus Security Act
25. seven
27. a
29. c
31. c
33. a
35. b
37. b
39. d
41. c
43. a
45. d

Chapter 3
1. False
3. False
5. True
7. False
9. True
11. True
13. False
15. False
17. scientific method
19. operationalized
21. self-selection
23. secondary analysis
25. negative/inverse
27. c
29. c
31. d
33. c
35. a
37. c
39. b

Chapter 4
1. True
3. False
5. False
7. True
9. False
11. False
13. True
15. *in se*
17. Edward the Confessor
19. useless
21. reducing anticipated reward
23. truth-in-sentencing
25. d
27. d
29. d
31. d
33. c
35. b
37. b
39. d

Chapter 5
1. True
3. True
5. False
7. False
9. True
11. False
13. False
15. False
17. constitutionally/genetically
19. scientific techniques
21. cycloids
23. enhancing
25. positive
27. monozygotic
29. b
31. b
33. b
35. d
37. a
39. a

Chapter 6
1. True
3. False
5. True
7. False
9. False
11. True
13. True
15. True
17. forensic psychiatry
19. biopsychology
21. sublimation
23. imitation
25. B.F. Skinner
27. defendant
29. c
31. b
33. b
35. a
37. a
39. c
41. d

Chapter 7
1. False
3. False
5. False
7. True
9. False
11. True
13. False
15. False
17. conflict
19. ethnographic
21. relative deprivation
23. socialization
25. reaction formation
27. a
29. a
31. d
33. a
35. d
37. b
39. a

Chapter 8
1. False
3. False
5. False
7. False
9. True
11. True

13. False
15. True
17. reinforcement
19. inner
21. secret
23. participation
25. ecological
27. b
29. c
31. c
33. c
35. c
37. b
39. d

Chapter 9
1. True
3. False
5. False
7. True
9. True
11. False
13. True
15. True
17. False
19. social control
21. political
23. instrumental
25. power-control
27. peace
29. c
31. a
33. b
35. b
37. b
39. a

Chapter 10
1. False
3. True
5. False
7. False
9. False
11. False
13. True
15. True
17. False
19. non-primary
21. mass
23. organized
25. power
27. assault
29. c
31. c
33. d
35. d
37. c
39. c

Chapter 11
1. True
3. False
5. True
7. False
9. False
11. True
13. True
15. True
17. False
19. automobiles
21. adolescents
23. 72
25. suitability
27. noncovered
29. b
31. b
33. b
35. a
37. b
39. a

Chapter 12
1. False
3. True
5. False
7. False
9. True
11. True
13. True
15. False
17. sophisticated
19. corporate
21. accountability
23. ethnic succession
25. underboss
27. Hobbs
29. b
31. c
33. a
35. c
37. c
39. b

Chapter 13
1. False
3. True
5. False
7. True
9. True
11. True
13. False
15. True
17. True
19. decreased
21. marijuana
23. pipelines
25. 1907
27. c
29. c
31. c
33. d
35. a
37. b
39. b

Chapter 14
1. False
3. False
5. True
7. False
9. True
11. False
13. False
15. True
17. trespass
19. virus
21. game players
23. British
25. Computer Fraud and Abuse
27. c
29. d
31. a
33. d
35. a
37. b
39. a

Chapter 15
1. False
3. True
5. False
7. True
9. True
11. False
13. False
15. False
17. Nixon
19. liberal
21. problems
23. instrumental use
25. cultural taboos
27. b
29. c
31. d
33. a
35. a
37. a
39. b

Chapter 16
1. True
3. False
5. False
7. True
9. True
11. cross-national
13. scenario writing
15. anomie
17. b
19. c
21. b